WHY LEADERS LIE

WHY LEADERS LIE
The Truth about Lying in International Politics

JOHN J. MEARSHEIMER

OXFORD
UNIVERSITY PRESS

2011

OXFORD
UNIVERSITY PRESS

Oxford University Press, Inc., publishes works that further
Oxford University's objective of excellence
in research, scholarship, and education.

Oxford   New York
Auckland   Cape Town   Dar es Salaam   Hong Kong   Karachi
Kuala Lumpur   Madrid   Melbourne   Mexico City   Nairobi
New Delhi   Shanghai   Taipei   Toronto

With offices in
Argentina   Austria   Brazil   Chile   Czech Republic   France   Greece
Guatemala   Hungary   Italy   Japan   Poland   Portugal   Singapore
South Korea   Switzerland   Thailand   Turkey   Ukraine   Vietnam

Copyright © 2011 by John J. Mearsheimer

Published by Oxford University Press, Inc.
198 Madison Avenue, New York, New York 10016
www.oup.com

Oxford is a registered trademark of Oxford University Press

Library of Congress Cataloging-in-Publication Data
Mearsheimer, John J.
Why leaders lie : the truth about lying in international politics /
John J. Mearsheimer.
    p. cm.
Includes bibliographical references and index.
ISBN-13: 978-0-19-975873-9 (hardcover : alk. paper)
ISBN-10: 0-19-975873-5
    1. International relations—Moral and ethical aspects.   2. Truthfulness and
falsehood—Political aspects.   3. Political ethics.   I. Title.
JZ1306.M43 2011
172'.4—dc22   2010013552

9 8 7 6 5 4 3 2 1

Printed in the United States of America
on acid-free paper

Contents

Preface

In the spring of 2003, Serge Schmemann of the *New York Times* called me out of the blue and said that he was working on a piece about lying in international politics for the Sunday paper's "Week in Review" section. He said that for some reason my name popped into his head, so he decided to call me. We had not met or talked before. I told him that I had never thought about the subject and I did not think there was much, if any, scholarly literature on international lying. I told him that he should tell me what he was thinking and I would react. We did just that and had what I thought was an interesting and fruitful discussion that lasted about an hour. Afterward, I wrote up some brief notes on the conversation and filed them away.

A few months later, in September 2003, I was invited to give a talk at MIT on a topic of my choosing. I thought it would be interesting to talk about lying in international politics, so I pulled up my notes from my conversation with Schmemann and crafted a talk for the occasion. Over the next six years, I wrote a paper, gave eight more talks, and had numerous conversations with friends and colleagues about this subject.

Throughout this process, I have been struck by the way people respond to the topic of international lying. Every audience and almost every person I have spoken to quickly becomes engaged and excited by the subject, and many want to talk at length about it. A number have sent me follow-up emails on their own initiative, including people who I have never met, but who were in the audience at one of my talks.

I can think of several reasons why this subject generates so much interest. For starters, most people consider lying to be a reprobate form of behavior, at least when you first broach the subject. Nearly everyone would recoil at being called a liar, even if they occasionally tell a lie themselves. Indeed, it is such a serious charge that people sometimes hesitate to call someone a liar even when they think the charge applies; instead they employ softer language. Senator John Kerry (D-MA), for example, was loath to call President Bush a liar during the 2004 presidential campaign and instead said that he "failed to tell the truth" about Iraq and "misled the American people."[1] However, the fact that lying is widely perceived to be wicked behavior is one reason that people like to talk about the subject. It gets the juices flowing.

What seems to make the subject even more interesting to many is that I argue that there are sometimes good strategic reasons for leaders to lie to other countries as well as to their own people. International lying, in other words, is not necessarily misconduct; in fact, it is often thought to be clever, necessary, and maybe even virtuous in some circumstances.

Yet no argument I make is more controversial and generates more discussion than my claim that statesmen and diplomats do not lie to each other very often. Hardly anyone seems to believe this is true—at least when they first hear it. Most people are surprisingly cynical on this issue. They seem to believe that there are countless examples where leaders around the world lied to each other and that therefore it should be easy to come up with a long list of those kinds of lies. In essence, they believe that inter-state lying is business as usual in international politics. I tell my interlocutors that as a card-carrying realist I was inclined at first to agree with them, but after studying the matter I have come to believe they are wrong. There is just not that much inter-state lying. Of course, this is not to say there is none.

The subject also resonates because of the Iraq war. Many well-informed people now believe that the Bush administration lied to the American people in the run-up to that conflict, which has turned into a strategic disaster for the United States. When a war goes badly and the public believes that deception helped make the war possible in the first place, people invariably get very interested in talking about why leaders would lie to their own citizens and what the likely consequences are. Plus the fact that there is hardly any literature on lying in international politics allows—or even compels—people to think creatively about these matters.

Given the dearth of literature on international lying and what seems to be a significant interest in the subject, I decided to turn my unpublished paper on lying into a book. My main aim was to provide some analytical frameworks that might help organize how we think about lying in international politics, as well as some theoretical claims about key aspects of that subject. I hope this book will be a conversation starter on an important topic that hitherto has received scant attention. If I am successful, others will follow in my footsteps and refine and challenge my arguments.

My thinking about lying has been markedly influenced by feedback from the audiences at the various places where I have spoken: the Council on Foreign Relations in New York; the Saltzman Institute of War and Peace Studies at Columbia University; the 2004 annual meeting of the American

Political Science Association; a faculty-student seminar at the University of Montana; the Browne Center for International Politics at the University of Pennsylvania; the MIT Political Science Department; the University of Chicago's Program on International Security Policy; the Lone Star National Security Forum; and the "North-South" workshop jointly run by the international-relations faculties of Northwestern University and the University of Chicago.

When I was in the early stages of organizing my thoughts on the subject, I benefited greatly from an informal seminar with five of my colleagues at the University of Chicago: Dong Sun Lee, Taka Nishi, Robert Pape, Sebastian Rosato, and John Schuessler. I am especially thankful for the extensive and especially useful comments provided by Alexander Downes, Sean Lynn-Jones, Marc Trachtenberg, and Stephen Walt, whose fingerprints are all over this manuscript.

Two other individuals deserve a special word of thanks. David McBride, my editor at Oxford University Press, made a number of very important suggestions that helped make the book better. I also deeply appreciate his enthusiasm for this project, which made it much easier to bring it across the finish line. But no person was more excited about it than my agent, Bill Clegg, who not only helped motivate me to complete the book, but also provided wise and indispensable counsel along the way.

I gratefully acknowledge the editorial expertise of Jessica Ryan and Ben Sadock at Oxford University Press, who helped so much to polish the final version. In addition, I received excellent comments and suggestions from two anonymous reviewers for the press and a long list of other individuals, some of whom I have never met. They include Eric Alterman, Stephen Ansolabehere, Robert Art, Richard Betts, David Blagden, Risa Brooks, Michael E. Brown, Jonathan Caverley, Joseph Cirincione, Michael Desch, Louis

DeScioli, Daniel Drezner, David Edelstein, Francis Gavin, Hein Goemans, Charles Glaser, Emily Goldman, Jennifer Hochschild, Ian Hurd, Robert Jervis, Chaim Kaufmann, Christopher Layne, Keir Lieber, Eric Lorber, Carlo Masala, Nuno Monteiro, Michael O'Connor, Joseph Parent, Susan Peterson, Arnd Plagge, Eric Posner, Richard Posner, Cynthia Roberts, Lawrence Samuels, David Schwartz, Jack Snyder, Ivan Arreguin-Toft, Monica Toft, Peter Toft, Matthew Tubin, Stephen Van Evera, Abraham Wagner, Alexander Wendt, and Joel Westra. My apologies to anyone I forgot.

I deeply appreciate everyone's help, as I could not have written this book without it. A special word of thanks is in order for Serge Schmemann, who introduced me to the subject of international lying and helped pique my interest in it. Of course, I bear full responsibility for all of the mistakes and foolish arguments, but owe a considerable debt to others for whatever insights this book contains.

Finally, I would like to thank my family, especially my wife, Pamela, for actually encouraging me to spend the endless hours that go into producing a book. I loved doing the research and writing anyway, but it is much easier when the people most affected by your work schedule fully support what you are trying to accomplish. Speaking of family, I would like to dedicate this book to my five wonderful children—Ann, Max, Nicholas, Julia, and David—who have been a source of great pride and pleasure for more than three decades.

WHY LEADERS LIE

Introduction

The key individuals in the Bush administration who pushed hard for the United States to invade Iraq before March 19, 2003 maintained that they were certain that Saddam Hussein had weapons of mass destruction (WMD). Their claims, they said, were based on hard evidence. Proponents of the war who were not in the administration frequently repeated those claims, creating a chorus of hawkish voices that helped convince many Americans that it was essential to disarm Iraq and depose Saddam. In this view, Iraq was a necessary war, not a war of choice. Anyone who doubted that claim was almost certain to be labeled an appeaser or a fool, or even accused of being unpatriotic. When no WMD were found in Iraq, those in the war party had to explain why they were so profoundly mistaken. How was it possible that so many who were so sure about Saddam's capabilities were so wrong?

One explanation offered for this blunder placed the blame squarely on Saddam, arguing that he effectively lied to us about whether Iraq had WMD. Specifically, he is said to have been deeply worried that Iran—or maybe even the United States—might attack Iraq, which had been badly weakened by its drubbing in the 1991 Gulf War as well as the sanctions and inspections regime that was imposed on Baghdad after that devastating defeat. To deter an attack on his country, so the story goes, Saddam put out false information that was designed to make Tehran and Washington think that he had WMD which he would use in the event of war. His job was made easier by the fact that the United Nations (UN) was not able to establish with a high degree of certainty that he no longer had any WMD, although it had no hard evidence that he possessed those weapons.

This line of argument is laid out in the "Duelfer Report," which was released in September 2004 by the Iraq Survey Group, an international team comprised of more than one thousand members that was tasked with finding Iraq's WMD stockpiles as well as the infrastructure used to build them. Former UN weapons inspector Charles A. Duelfer led it. After describing the various threats facing Iraq, the report tells us, "in order to counter these threats, Saddam continued with his public posture of retaining the WMD capability."[1] The report goes on to say: "While it appears that Iraq, by the mid-1990s, was essentially free of militarily significant WMD stocks, Saddam's perceived requirement to bluff about WMD capabilities made it too dangerous to clearly reveal this to the international community, especially Iran." George Tenet makes the same argument in his memoirs. He writes in *At the Center of the Storm*: "We had no previous experience with a country that did not possess such weapons but pretended that it did....Before the war, we didn't understand that *he* was bluffing."[2]

These claims notwithstanding, there is no evidence in the public record that Saddam tried to convince the world that Iraq possessed WMD. The Duelfer report, for example, furnishes no proof to support its claim about the Iraqi leader's bluffing. That claim is merely an assertion, and the authors of the report do not provide facts to back it up. Indeed, the report itself provides evidence that casts doubts on that contention. It notes "Saddam never discussed using deception as a policy," and that one of his most trusted deputies stated that he "did not reveal he was deceiving the world about the presence of WMD."[3] This is hardly surprising, since there is no evidence that he was deceiving the world. In fact, he said on a number of occasions that he had no WMD and he was telling the truth.[4]

The Bush administration, on the other hand, told four major lies in the run-up to the Iraq War. They are all discussed in detail below, but let me briefly summarize them here. Key figures in the administration falsely claimed that they knew with complete certainty that Iraq had WMD. They also lied when they said that they had foolproof evidence that Saddam was closely allied with Osama bin Laden, and they made various statements that falsely implied that Saddam bore some responsibility for the September 11 attacks on the United States. Finally, various individuals in the administration, including President Bush himself, claimed that they were still open to peaceful resolution of their dispute with Saddam, when in fact the decision to go to war had already been made.

In short, Saddam told the truth about his WMD capabilities before the 2003 Iraq war, while senior figures in the Bush administration lied about what they knew regarding those weapons. They also lied about some other important matters. This behavior by the two sides might seem surprising, maybe even shocking, to some readers. One might think that at the very least it is a highly unusual case. But that conclusion would be wrong. Both sides acted in ways that are consistent with two of the main findings in this book.

Specifically, I find that leaders do not lie very often to other countries, but instead seem more inclined to lie to their own people. Let me explain.

Although lying is widely viewed as reprehensible behavior in ordinary life, it is acceptable conduct in international politics because there are sometimes good strategic reasons for leaders to lie to other countries and even to their own people. Nevertheless, there is actually not much lying between states. When I began this study, I expected to find abundant evidence of statesmen and diplomats lying to each other. But that initial assumption turned out to be wrong. Instead, I had to work hard to find the cases of international lying that I discuss in this book. Leaders do lie to other countries on occasion, but much less often than one might think. Therefore, it is not surprising that Saddam Hussein did not lie about whether he had WMD before the Iraq War, which is not to say that there are no circumstances in which he would have lied.

Furthermore, leaders appear to be more likely to lie to their own people about foreign policy issues than to other countries. That certainly seems to be true for democracies that pursue ambitious foreign policies and are inclined to initiate wars of choice, i.e., when there is not a clear and imminent danger to a country's vital interests that can only be dealt with by force. Of course, that description fits the United States over the past seventy years, and, not surprisingly, American presidents have told their fellow citizens a number of important lies about foreign policy matters over those seven decades. Thus, it is hardly surprising that key figures in the Bush administration—including the president himself—lied to the American people in the run-up to the Iraq War. Bush was following in the footsteps of illustrious predecessors like Franklin D. Roosevelt, who lied about a naval incident in 1941 to help draw the United States into

World War II, and Lyndon B. Johnson, who lied about events in the Gulf of Tonkin in the summer of 1964 so that he could get congressional support to wage war against North Vietnam.

It is important to emphasize that in none of those cases were the president or his lieutenants lying for narrow personal gain. They thought that they were acting in the American national interest, which is not to say they acted wisely in every case. But the fact is that there are good strategic reasons for leaders to lie to their publics as well as to other countries. These practical logics almost always override well-known and widely accepted moral strictures against lying. Indeed, leaders sometimes think that they have a moral duty to lie to protect their country. Leaders do not always lie about foreign policy, of course, but they occasionally say things or purposely imply things that they know are not true. Their publics usually do not punish them for their deceptions, however, unless they lead to bad results. It seems clear that leaders and their publics believe that lying is an integral part of international relations.

In domestic politics, however, lying is generally considered wrong, save for some special circumstances, such as when individuals are bargaining over the price at which they would buy or sell a house, or when protecting an innocent person from wrongful harm. Most people consider "white lies" that friends tell one another—as when dinner guests praise an ill-cooked meal, or that parents tell their children to protect them—permissible. After all, these sorts of lies involve small stakes and they are told for someone else's benefit.[5] They are altruistic lies. But on the whole, lying is widely seen to have a corrupting effect on individuals as well as the broader society in which they live. It is not surprising, therefore, that people often tell the truth even when it is not in their material interest to do so.[6] This is not to deny that there is a good deal of lying of the unacceptable sort in every society. Still, the less of that there is the better.[7] Thus, it makes good sense to stigmatize and discourage lying on the home front.

There is a simple explanation for these different attitudes toward domestic and international lying. A leader has no higher obligation than to ensure the survival of his country. Yet states operate in an anarchic system where there is no higher authority that they can turn to if they are seriously threatened by another state. In the harsh world of international politics, there is no 911 number to call if a state gets in trouble, and even if there were, there is nobody at the other end to pick up the phone. Thus, leaders and their publics understand that states operate in a self-help world where they have to do whatever is necessary to provide for their own security. If that means lying and cheating, so be it. International politics, in other words, tends to be a realm where rules are often broken with little consequence. This is not to say that leaders are enthusiastic about telling lies or to deny that many leaders would prefer to see the international realm governed by a well-defined set of moral principles. But that is not feasible in the absence of a common sovereign to enforce them.

In contrast to the international system, the structure of a state is hierarchic, not anarchic.[8] In a well-ordered state, there is a higher authority—the state itself—to which individuals can turn for protection. Consequently, the incentives to cheat and lie that apply when states are dealing with each other usually do not apply to individuals within a state. Indeed, a strong case can be made that widespread lying threatens the inner life of a state. It does so in good part for purely utilitarian reasons, as it is hard to make a state function efficiently when people lie to each other all the time. One can also make a moral case against lying within the confines of a state, because a well-defined community usually exists there, which is not the case in international politics. Thomas Hobbes put the point succinctly in *Leviathan*: "Before the names of Just, and Unjust can have place, there must be some coercive Power to compel men equally to the performance of their Covenants.... Where there is no Common-wealth, there nothing is Unjust."[9]

Lying is obviously a form of deception, but not all deception is lying. There are two other kinds of deception: concealment and spinning. Unlike lying, neither involves making a false statement or telling a story with a false bottom line. Concealment and spinning, however, are not the same as telling the truth.

These two kinds of deception are pervasive in every realm of daily life, and they cause hardly a word of protest.[10] For example, a person interviewing for a job is allowed to spin his life story on a resume in ways that present him in the most favorable light. He is free to omit information from that resume as he sees fit.[11] Politics is an especially fertile breeding ground for spinning and concealing. A president can tell a story about the state of the American economy that accentuates the positive trends and downplays or even ignores the negative ones, while a critic from the opposing party is free to do the opposite. But neither individual is allowed to lie to make his case. Indeed, getting caught in a lie would probably do them significant political harm.

That is not true, however, if a foreign-policy issue is at stake. Statesmen and diplomats are rarely punished for lying, especially if they were telling lies to other countries. Probably the only exception to this rule involves cases where it becomes known that a leader lied to his fellow citizens about a policy that failed in ways that obviously damage the national interest. But even here, the main reason that a leader would likely incur his public's wrath is because the policy failed, not because he lied. Of course, this is why a leader who is discovered to have lied to his public about a particular policy is unlikely to pay much of a political price if it works as intended. When it comes to foreign policy, success excuses lying, or at least makes it tolerable.

In short, concealment and spinning are generally seen as legitimate forms of behavior in domestic as well as international politics. Buy lying is a different matter.[12] It is considered unacceptable behavior in most walks of life, save for international politics, where it is generally viewed as regrettable but sometimes necessary.

THE TASK AHEAD

There is a substantial body of literature on lying, but hardly any of it deals explicitly with lying in international politics. One notable exception is Eric Alterman's *When Presidents Lie: A History of Official Deception and Its Consequences,* which provides an excellent narrative of presidential lying over the past seventy years.[13] However, Alterman is not a social scientist and he does not attempt to theorize about international lying. Nor has anyone else. One might respond that there are numerous studies dealing with deception among states. While this is true, that literature tends not to distinguish between concealment, lying, and spinning, and more importantly, no work zeroes in on lying and attempts to make general arguments about that particular behavior. The aim of this book is to fill that void by theorizing about international lying, not the broader concept of deception.

At the most general level, one can think about lying from either an absolutist or a utilitarian perspective. Absolutists like Immanuel Kant and Augustine maintain that lying is always wrong and that it has hardly any positive effects. Lying, according to Kant, is "the greatest violation of man's duty to himself."[14] Utilitarians, on the other hand, believe that lying sometimes makes sense, because it serves a useful social purpose; but other times it does not. The key is to determine when and why lying has positive utility.

I look at international lying from a strictly utilitarian perspective, mainly because there are compelling reasons that justify it and, not surprisingly, we find a considerable amount of it in the historical record. Many people seem to believe that there are circumstances in world politics where it pays to lie. This is not to deny, however, the importance of examining the moral dimensions of this phenomenon. Nevertheless, that task involves a different set of calculations and considerations, which lie beyond the scope of this book.

Broadly speaking, leaders tell international lies for two different reasons. They can tell lies in the service of the national interest. These are *strategic lies* that leaders tell for the purpose of helping their country survive in the rough and tumble of inter-state relations. Leaders can also tell *selfish lies,* which have little to do with raison d'état, but instead aim to protect their own personal interests or those of their friends. My concern is with lies that leaders tell for the good of the collectivity, not for selfish purposes. Thus, when I use the term international lying, I am talking about strategic lies, not selfish lies.

The subsequent analysis is built around four questions. First, what are the different kinds of international lies that leaders tell? Second, why do they lie? What are the strategic logics that motivate each kind of lying? Specifically, what are the potential benefits of lying that cause leaders to engage in this distasteful, if not noxious, behavior? Third, what are the circumstances that make each type of lying more or less likely? Fourth, what are the potential costs of lying for a state's domestic politics as well as its foreign policy? In other words, what is the downside of telling international lies? Thus, I consider both the benefits and the costs of the various kinds of lies that statesmen and diplomats tell each other as well as their own publics. However, I do not address the important question of when each kind of lie is likely to achieve its intended effect or not, mainly because I could not come up with a good answer.

I attempt to answer these questions by providing simple analytical frameworks that draw on the theoretical literature in international relations as well as the extensive literature on lying. I have tried to ensure that my arguments are logically sound, and I have provided historical evidence to illustrate them. However, I do not test my various claims by bringing evidence to bear in a systematic manner. That task is beyond the scope of this book, which is mainly concerned with providing a theoretical template for thinking about international lying. I hope other scholars will systematically test some of the arguments offered in the following pages.

THE MAIN ARGUMENTS AND THE ROAD MAP

I make numerous claims in the subsequent analysis, but five of them stand out above the rest. First, international lying comes in a variety of forms, but the most important distinction is between the lies that states tell each other and those that leaders tell their own publics.

Second, leaders usually tell international lies for good strategic reasons, not because they are craven or corrupt. Lest I be misunderstood, I am not saying that lying is a great virtue and that more international lying is better than less. I am merely saying that lying is sometimes a useful instrument of statecraft in a dangerous world. Indeed, a leader can occasionally tell what Plato famously called a "noble lie." For example, President Franklin Roosevelt lied to the American people about the German attack on the USS *Greer* in August

1941. He was trying to get the United States into World War II against Nazi Germany, which then appeared to be on its way to conquering all of Europe. Roosevelt's objective was the right one and it was appropriate for him to lie in this instance.

Third, while lying among states is a permanent fixture of international politics, it is not commonplace. In the discussion of inter-state lying in chapter 3, I describe a variety of cases in which the leaders of one state lied to another state. Reading this chapter might give the impression that inter-state lying is routine behavior among statesmen and diplomats. But I had difficulty finding those cases, and, moreover, the chapter includes almost all the cases I was able to identify. I was especially surprised by how difficult it was to find evidence of states attempting to bluff each other in bargaining situations.[15] In fact, it appears that leaders are more likely to lie to their own people than to rival states. That seems to be particularly true for democracies like the United States.

Fourth, the most dangerous kinds of international lies are those that leaders tell their own citizens. They are more likely to backfire and damage a state's strategic position than the lies that leaders tell other states. Moreover, they are more likely to corrupt political and social life at home, which can have many harmful consequences for daily life.

Fifth, because the United States is so powerful and so heavily engaged around the globe, its leaders often confront situations where there are strong incentives to lie either to other states or to the American people. This is a matter of serious concern, since international lying can have serious negative consequences, especially for democracies like the United States.

This book is comprised of nine chapters. I start by defining lying and the other two forms of deception: concealment and spinning. The subsequent chapter lays out the inventory of international lies. I distinguish between strategic lies and selfish lies, and explain why the focus is on the former kind. In the next five chapters, I look in detail at each of the different kinds of strategic lies. I consider the logic behind each type and when it is more or less likely to occur. In the penultimate chapter, I consider the potential pitfalls of international lying. I assess which kinds of lies are most likely to backfire and undermine a state's foreign policy and which are most likely to cause damage on the home front. I conclude with a brief discussion of what all of this means for American foreign policy and the United States more generally.

CHAPTER 1

What is Lying?

Before defining lying, spinning, and concealment, it makes good sense to define deception, the general category that includes those three behaviors, as well as truth telling, which is the direct opposite of deception.

Truth telling is when an individual does his best to state the facts and tell a story in a straightforward and honest way. Every person invariably has limited knowledge about the details of any case and biases as well. Memories can also be faulty and it is impossible to relate every fact one knows when telling a story. The key point, however, is that a truth teller makes a serious effort to overcome any biases or selfish interests that he might have and report the relevant facts in as fair-minded a way as he can. *Deception,* in contrast, is where an individual purposely takes steps that are designed to prevent others from knowing the full truth—as that individual understands it—about a particular matter. The deliberate aim, in other words, is not to provide a straightforward or comprehensive description of events.

Lying is when a person makes a statement that he knows or suspects to be false in the hope that others will think it is true. A lie is a positive action designed to deceive the target audience. Lying can involve making up facts that one knows to be false or denying facts that one knows to be true. But lying is not only about the truthfulness of particular facts. It can also involve the disingenuous arrangement of facts to tell a fictitious story. Specifically, a person is lying when he uses facts—even true facts—to imply that something is true, when he knows that it is not true.[1] In such cases, the liar is purposely leading the listener to a false conclusion without explicitly stating that conclusion.

There is always the possibility, of course, that a person who thinks that he is telling a lie has the facts wrong and is inadvertently telling the truth. The reverse might be true as well: a person who believes that he is telling the truth might have his facts wrong. This problem, however, is irrelevant for my purposes, because I am interested in determining whether a person is being truthful—stating facts or telling a story that he believes to be true—not whether he ultimately proves to be right or wrong about the facts. Simply put, my concern is with truthfulness, not the truth.[2]

Spinning is different from lying, although there will be some cases where the distinction is murky. Spinning is when a person telling a story emphasizes certain facts and links them together in ways that play to his advantage, while, at the same time, downplaying or ignoring inconvenient facts. Spinning is all about interpreting the known facts in a way that allows the spinner to tell a favorable story. It is all about emphasizing and deemphasizing particular facts to portray one's position in a positive light. With spinning, no attempt is made to render a completely accurate account of events. The basic story being told is distorted, but the facts are not put together so as to tell a false story, which would be a lie. Spinning is exaggeration or distortion, not prevarication. Tiger Woods captured the essence of spinning when he told an interviewer from *Sports Illustrated* in 2000, "I've learned you can always tell the truth, but you don't have to tell the whole truth."[3]

What usually happens in an American courtroom provides a good way of illustrating the difference between lying and spinning. When a witness is called to the stand he is sworn to tell "the truth, the whole truth and nothing but the truth" and then he is asked a series of questions, which he is expected to answer truthfully. The person in the docket could lie, but the key point is that he is required by law to tell what he believes to be the truth. The attorneys for the plaintiff and the defendant, on the other hand, are primarily interested in winning the case for their clients, not determining the full truth about what happened in the dispute at hand. Accordingly, each makes an opening and closing statement in which he spins the facts of the case in ways that puts his client in the most favorable light. The rival lawyers invariably tell two different stories, but neither is allowed to lie. The American Bar Association, for example, stipulates in its rules of conduct that "a lawyer shall not knowingly make a false statement of fact or law to a tribunal."[4] Spinning, however, is not only permissible; it is what lawyers routinely do for their clients.

The third kind of deception is *concealment,* which involves withholding information that might undermine or weaken one's position. In cases of this sort, the individual simply remains silent about the evidence, because he wants to hide it from others. Of course, if he is asked a question about the matter and lies to conceal it, that behavior fits my definition of lying. A good example of concealment is the Bush administration's decision not to tell the public before the Iraq War began in March 2003 that two key Al Qaeda figures—Khalid

Sheikh Mohammed and Abu Zabaydah—had separately told their American interrogators that Osama bin Laden had thought about asking Saddam Hussein to form an alliance against the United States, but then decided against it.[5] If these facts had been made public, they would have undermined the Bush administration's claim that bin Laden and Saddam were collaborating with each other, which was important for winning public and congressional support for the war. This behavior was certainly deceptive, but it was not lying, at least according to my definition, because it did not involve taking a positive step to deceive someone.[6] In short, when a person spins a story or conceals facts, he is not lying, but neither is he being completely truthful.

Lying, as emphasized, is usually considered deplorable behavior, whereas most people seem to believe that it is acceptable to spin and conceal, even though these behaviors are designed to deceive. One possible reason for this difference is that lying is more difficult to detect and protect against than either spinning or concealment. Liars make false assertions in ways that are designed not to raise any doubts about the truthfulness of their claims. Skillful liars present false assertions with an air of certainty that makes it especially difficult for the target audience to figure out that it is being bamboozled.

With spinning, however, the listeners are much more likely to be able to recognize that they are not getting a complete and accurate picture, and then rectify the problem by filling in the missing pieces of the story. Specifically, the target audience can compare the spinner's motives with how the spinner put his story together, i.e., what he might have left out, what he emphasized, and what he deemphasized. If there is reason to be suspicious of the spinner's story, the listeners can ask the spinner for additional information, do independent research on the spinner's story, or listen to counter-spinners, who are usually not in short supply when it comes to foreign policy.

The target audience should also be able to defend itself reasonably well against concealment. In particular, it can always ask if there is information available on specific aspects of the subject at hand, and it should expect to be told the truth. None of this is to deny, however, that the target audience might not know all the relevant lines of inquiry. After all, sometimes you do not know what you do not know, and therefore do not know what questions to ask.

To reinforce the point that lying is considered shameful because it is so difficult to detect, let us look at one of the few realms in our daily life where it is acceptable to lie: commercial negotiations where buyers and sellers are trying to reach a price agreement. Consider, for example, a case in which two individuals are bargaining over a commodity like a car or a house. Each person is allowed to lie about his "reservation price," which is the price above or below which he would no longer agree to a deal. Both the buyer and the seller understand that lying—the euphemism is "bluffing"—is part of the game; thus neither side gains an unfair advantage when it lies about the selling price or the purchase price. In essence, we are talking about a fair fight in which neither side can claim that it was wrongly bamboozled by the other side.

Not surprisingly, there is hardly any stigma attached to lying about one's reservation price in business dealings. Indeed, one might argue that this kind of bluffing is not lying, because, to quote the British statesman Henry Taylor, a "falsehood ceases to be a falsehood when it is understood on all sides that the truth is not expected to be spoken."[7] I reject that logic, however, because both the buyer and seller are telling falsehoods that are intended to deceive the other side, which is the essence of lying.

In sum, lying, spinning, and withholding information are all forms of deception, and all three can be contrasted with truth telling. The subsequent discussion focuses on how lies are used to deceive others in the foreign-policy realm. But in practice, deception campaigns invariably involve spinning and concealment as well as lying. In fact, given the opprobrium attached to most kinds of lying, leaders who think that they have good reason to deceive another state or their own public usually prefer spinning and concealment to lying. Nobody wants to be called a liar, even if it is for a good cause. This preference is reinforced by the fact that it is often difficult to lie without getting caught red-handed. Of course, leaders sometimes conclude that they have no choice but to lie for their countries and that circumstances make it feasible to do so. In general, however, lying will be the option of last resort for leaders seeking to deceive another country.

Let us now consider the various kinds of lies that are told in international politics.

CHAPTER 2

The Inventory of International Lies

In the foreign policy realm, leaders can tell seven different kinds of lies. Each type serves a specific purpose, although a single lie can serve multiple purposes. For example, a lie that a leader tells his people about a foreign threat to generate public support for countering it (fearmongering) might also help foster nationalism on the home front by portraying the adversary in an especially harsh light (nationalist mythmaking). This particular kind of lie is aimed at the policymaker's own public, but lies can also be beamed at rival states as well as allies. However, a lie directed at any one of these audiences will invariably reach the others, which might have positive or negative consequences.

Inter-state lies are aimed directly at other countries either for the purpose of gaining a strategic advantage over them or preventing them from gaining an advantage at your expense. This type of lie is usually directed at rival states, but states sometimes lie to their allies. Leaders engaged in inter-state lying usually end up deceiving their own people, although they are not the intended audience.

Fearmongering occurs when a leader lies to his own people about a foreign-policy threat that he believes they do not recognize or fully appreciate. The aim is to motivate the public to take the threat seriously and make the necessary sacrifices to counter it. Leaders do not fearmonger because they are evil or because they are pursuing selfish gains, but because they believe that inflating a particular threat serves the national interest.

Strategic cover-ups are lies designed to hide either failed policies or controversial policies from the public and some-times from other states as well. Leaders do not tell these lies to protect incompetents who bungled their job or to con-ceal foolish policies—although that can be an unintended consequence. The aim instead is to protect the country from harm. For example, lying to the public about military incom-petence in wartime is sometimes important for maintaining solidarity on the home front, which can mean the difference between defeat and victory.

Nationalist mythmaking is when leaders tell lies, mainly to their own people, about their country's past.[1] In essence, they tell a story in which "we" are always right and "they" are always wrong. Elites do this by denying that their nation or ethnic group has done things it has actually done or by falsely claiming that it has done certain things it has not done. Of course, those elites tell a similar set of lies about rival groups. The purpose is to create a powerful sense of group identity among the broader population, because that is necessary for building and maintaining a viable nation-state, and for motivating people to fight wars for their homeland. These myths sometimes help states gain legitimacy with other states.

Liberal lies are designed to cover up the behavior of states when it contradicts the well-developed body of lib-eral norms that is widely accepted around the world and codified in international law. Countries of all kinds, including liberal democracies, sometimes act brutally toward other states, or form alliances with particularly odious states. When that happens, a state's leaders will usually invent a story for their people—or the wider world—that tries to disguise their illiberal actions with idealistic rhetoric.

Social imperialism occurs when leaders tell lies about another country for the purpose of promoting either their own economic or political interests or those of a particular social class or interest group. The aim is to divert the public's attention from problems or controversies on the home front in ways that will benefit a narrow slice of society, not the general welfare. For example, leaders might try to solidify their hold on power by exaggerating a threat and creating fear on the home front, which, in turn, will lead the public to rally around the regime.

Ignoble cover-ups are when leaders lie about their blunders or unsuccessful policies for self-serving reasons. Their main aim is to protect themselves or their friends from well-deserved punishment.[2] This kind of lie is not designed to benefit the wider public, which is the main purpose of a strategic cover-up. Nevertheless, because strategic cover-ups usually end up protecting the incompetent, it is sometimes difficult to distinguish between these two kinds of cover-ups.

These seven varieties of falsehoods largely encompass the universe of international lies.[3] However, the subsequent discussion concentrates on lies that are told in the service of the national interest. These strategic lies benefit the collectivity, unlike selfish lies, which benefit a particular individual or group of individuals. In practice, this means that there will be no further discussion of either social imperialism or ignoble cover-ups.

These two types of falsehoods are omitted because there is no good strategic justification for them. Of course, we know why individuals tell lies of this sort, but hardly anyone would argue that they are legitimate forms of behavior. Indeed, most observers would condemn these selfish lies, not only because they have a corrupting influence on political life, but also because they jeopardize the broader national interest. In short, social imperialism and ignoble cover-ups have no redeeming social value.

Strategic lies are a different matter. They aim to facilitate the general welfare and they usually have at least a modicum of legitimacy. In essence, strategic lies can do good things for a country, although there is always the possibility that they will do more harm than good. The focus here is on the five kinds of strategic falsehoods described above: inter-state lies, fearmongering, strategic cover-ups, nationalist mythmaking, and liberal lies. In addition to describing each type in greater detail, I will lay out the underlying causal logics and explain when each is more or less likely to occur. In other words, I will explain why and when you get these different kinds of international lies.

CHAPTER 3

Lying between States

Sir Henry Wotton, the seventeenth-century British diplomat, once remarked that an ambassador is "an honest man sent to lie abroad for the good of his country."[1] This comment nicely captures the fact that states do lie to each other, because they think that lying serves the national interest. Wotton's remark, however, is misleading in the sense that it implies that diplomats and statesmen routinely spend their time lying to each other. In fact, political leaders and their diplomatic representatives tell each other the truth far more often than they lie. Even when they are bent on deceiving one another, they are more likely to rely on concealment rather than overt lying. Secrecy, as virtually all students of international politics know well, is a time-honored approach to developing weapons and strategies that can give one country an advantage over its rivals.

On what basis do I make these claims? As noted, I am not testing my arguments by systematically examining them in light of the historical record. In fact, I am not sure that it is possible to measure how often statesmen and diplomats have lied to each other in the past as compared to how often they have been truthful with each other. One reason is that over past centuries there have a vast number of interactions among the leaders of the different political units that have comprised the international system. It is difficult to see how one could select a representative sample of cases from that immense database. But even if that were feasible, it would still be impossible to investigate what transpired in many of those cases. We have only sparse records of what happened in the distant past, and even in more recent cases, the records are sometimes incomplete. For these same reasons, it would also be especially difficult—maybe impossible—to determine precisely how much inter-state lying has gone on as opposed to concealing and spinning.

My claim that there has not been much inter-state lying over time is based on two considerations. First, I had difficulty finding examples of leaders lying to each other, although I certainly found some cases, most of which are discussed below. I also asked other scholars who are well versed in international history if they could provide me with examples of statesmen and diplomats lying to one another. Their initial reaction—like mine—was that there must be an abundance of such cases; but in the end virtually everyone I approached had trouble finding more than a few clear-cut cases of inter-state lying.

Of course, one's definition of lying affects any assessment of how much lying there has been among states, or any other kind of lying, for that matter. Sissela Bok, for example, notes in her important treatise on lying that some people define the concept of lying so broadly that they "take all forms of deception to be lies, regardless of whether or not they involve statements of any kind." When this expansive definition is employed, people can then say that lying is rampant in daily life, and "that the average person lies ten, twenty, a hundred times a day."[2]

If applied to international politics, this definition of lying would include spinning and concealment, as well as consciously telling a deliberate untruth, and one could therefore say that inter-state lying was commonplace. But if one defines lying more narrowly, as Bok and I do, it is not nearly as widespread, although it is surely not unknown. I believe a narrower definition makes more sense, because it allows us to discriminate between different forms of deception and to theorize about when and why each may be employed.

One might argue that statesmen and diplomats who lie to each other are not going to admit it, and indeed are likely to go to some lengths to hide it. Perhaps there are numerous cases of inter-state lying, but I have failed to uncover most of them because they are well-hidden from those who were not involved in the decision-making process. This line of argument certainly has some merit when analyzing contemporary events, since important information is almost always concealed from the public, and it is therefore hard for outsiders to know what transpired behind closed doors. Also, the further back in history we go, the more incomplete the records are about the policymaking process in virtually every country, which means that inter-state lying might have been commonplace long ago, but we cannot expose it. There are even some recent cases where the historical record is spotty, which again raises the possibility of deeply buried lies.

Still, I do not think there are many well-concealed inter-state lies lurking in the past. I base this claim on the fact that we do have plenty of information on many important foreign-policy decisions made over the past two centuries by a variety of countries, which would make it difficult for leaders to hide their lies so well that they would never be discovered. This would be especially true for lies that had a major impact on a country's foreign policy. After all, a deliberate deception campaign usually involves many people, and at least some of them are bound to talk eventually. Plus, the written records, which are extensive in many of these cases, have now come to light. Thus, most of the key details of many recent historical events have become public—including the lies. This is not to deny that a few well-told lies from the past might have escaped detection, but it is hard to imagine that there are many such cases.

There is a second reason why I think that inter-state lying has been uncommon: it is usually difficult to bamboozle another country's leaders. Even when it is feasible, the costs of lying often outweigh the benefits. In other words, there are compelling reasons why we should not expect lying among states to be commonplace.

For starters, basic realist logic explains why it is difficult for leaders to get away with lying to other countries when important strategic issues are at stake. States operating in an anarchic system have powerful incentives to sometimes act in ruthless and deceitful ways to ensure their survival, and this repertoire of possible tactics surely includes lying. Former Israeli prime minister Yitzhak Shamir captured this point when he said, "For the sake of the Land of Israel it's all right to lie."[3] Not surprisingly, almost all leaders, and even many of their citizens, recognize that international relations are governed in large part by a different set of rules than those which govern daily life inside their country. Thus, when it comes to important matters of state, they are unlikely to trust pronouncements by another government unless they can verify them.[4] As former president Ronald Reagan famously warned, "Trust, but verify." No Western leader, for example, is going to accept Iran's claim that it is not developing nuclear weapons and leave the issue there. Instead, they will insist that the International Atomic Energy Agency be able to inspect Iran's nuclear facilities to make sure that it is not trying to acquire nuclear weapons.

The problem is especially acute when assessing another country's intentions, which are difficult to determine with a high degree of confidence. It is much easier, although not necessarily easy, to count and assess another country's military capabilities, which are tangible assets that can be seen by the naked eye. Intentions, on the other hand, are ultimately in the minds of policymakers, making them impossible to observe and measure, which ultimately works to diminish trust between states. Given this general lack of trust, it is difficult for leaders to get away with lying to each other when the stakes are high. Thus it is not surprising that the historical record contains hardly any examples of devastatingly effective inter-state lies.

Statesmen and diplomats are more likely to trust each other when they are dealing with issues where there would be no major strategic consequences if either side fell for a lie. In other words, leaders are usually less likely to worry about being deceived when the issue at hand involves economics or the environment—"low politics"—as opposed to national security—"high politics"—where trust is scarce.[5] One might think that there would be a significant amount of lying when low politics are at play, because leaders are likely to be more trusting and thus more vulnerable to being duped. But that is not the case; there is not much inter-state lying even when the stakes are relatively low.

One reason why there is not much lying when low politics are at play is that the gains from deceiving another country are likely to be small. Of course, that is why the potential victim is vulnerable to lying: the stakes are low and thus the costs of being bamboozled are not great, so the victim lets his guard down. Another reason is that if statesmen were inveterate liars, nobody would believe anything they said, which would rob lying of its effect. Lying is only effective when the potential victim thinks that the liar is probably telling the truth. Thus, there has to be good reason for leaders to think that they are not being misled, which means that they cannot lie to each other too often without rendering lying ineffective. In short, inter-state lying must be done selectively and carefully to be useful.

A final reason is that if leaders often lied to each other, it would be almost impossible for them to interact in constructive ways, since nobody would know what to think was true or false. And if a particular leader frequently lied, he would surely get a reputation for dishonesty, and other leaders would be reluctant to reach future agreements with him, which might seriously hurt his country. This is especially true when dealing with economic and environmental issues where there is the promise of continued cooperation in the years ahead. Too much lying, in other words, is bad for business.

All of this is to say that lying has its limits as a tool of statecraft.

WHY STATES LIE TO EACH OTHER

The main reason that leaders lie to foreign audiences is to gain a strategic advantage for their country. Because states operate in an anarchic world, where there is no night watchman to protect them in case of serious trouble, they have no choice but to provide for their own security. The best way that states can maximize their prospects for survival is to gain power at their rivals' expense. However, they can also use deception, which includes lying, to achieve an advantage over a potential adversary. In a dangerous world, leaders do what they must to insure their country's survival. Arthur Sylvester, the assistant secretary of defense for public affairs during the Kennedy administration, captured this point when he said, in the wake of the Cuban Missile Crisis, "I think the inherent right of the Government to lie to save itself when faced with nuclear disaster is basic."[6] Some twenty years later, President Jimmy Carter's press secretary, Jody Powell, remarked, "But Sylvester, of course, was right. In certain circumstances, government not only has the right but a positive obligation to lie."[7]

In practice, inter-state lying takes different forms and operates according to different logics. Let us consider some of the ways in which states lie to each other. This list is not meant to be exhaustive, although most inter-state lies would fit into one of these categories.

First, leaders sometimes exaggerate their state's capabilities for purposes of deterring an adversary, or maybe even coercing it. For example, Hitler lied about German military capabilities during the 1930s. He tried to inflate the Wehrmacht's strength so as to discourage Britain and France from interfering with German rearmament as well as his aggressive foreign policy moves, like the remilitarization of the Rhineland in 1936.[8] In roughly the same period, Josef Stalin's infamous purges did serious damage to the fighting power of the Red Army. Worried that this might make the Soviet Union look weak and invite an attack from Nazi Germany, Stalin and his lieutenants put out the word that the Soviet military was a formidable fighting force, when they knew it was not.[9]

Another instance of this kind of inter-state lying occurred during the Cold War, after the Soviets launched the first-ever intercontinental ballistic missile (ICBM) in October 1957.[10] The strategic nuclear balance at the time clearly favored the United States. Soviet Premier Nikita Khrushchev took advantage of his country's early lead in ICBMs to claim that the Soviet Union had an ICBM capability that was far greater than what they actually had. Khrushchev's lying over the next three years contributed to the famous myth of the "missile gap," in which the United States was thought to be at a serious disadvantage in terms of strategic missiles. In fact, the opposite was true: the Soviet Union had far fewer ICBMs than the United States. Khrushchev's reason for exaggerating Soviet capabilities was to deter as well as coerce the United States. In particular, he wanted to make sure that the Americans did not launch a strategic nuclear strike against the Soviet Union in a crisis. He was also determined to put great pressure on the Eisenhower administration to abandon its plans to allow Germany to acquire nuclear weapons.

A second kind of inter-state lie is when a leader tells false-hoods for the purpose of minimizing the importance of a particular military capability, or even hiding it from rival countries. The deceiver's aim might be to avoid provoking an attack aimed at destroying that capability, or to prevent another state from forcing it to give up that capability. For example, after Admiral Alfred von Tirpitz became the head of the German navy in June 1897, he set out to build a fleet that could challenge British naval supremacy and allow Germany to pursue its ambitious *Weltpolitik*.[11] He realized, however, that the German Navy would be vulnerable to a British attack in the early stages of its development; he referred to this as "the danger zone." To prevent that outcome, he and other German leaders launched a propaganda campaign in which they falsely claimed that Berlin was building a fleet for defensive purposes—to protect Germany's growing overseas trade—and that they had no intention of challenging the British navy.

Israel lied to the United States in the 1960s about its nascent nuclear weapons program because it feared that Washington would force the Jewish state to shut down the project if it acknowledged what was really going on at the

Dimona nuclear complex. "This is one program," Henry Kissinger wrote in 1969, "on which the Israelis have persistently deceived us."[12] Another case in point was when the Soviets placed offensive missiles in Cuba in 1963 after they had repeatedly assured the Kennedy administration that they would not take that dangerous step. Their hope was to present the president "with a fait accompli at some moment of Khrushchev's choice," without giving Kennedy reason to move against them before the missiles were installed.[13]

A state might also downplay or hide its military capabilities to minimize the chances that an adversary would counter them either by altering its strategy, building defenses, or racing to build more of the same kind of weapons. During World War I, for example, Britain secretly developed the tank to help break the stalemate on the Western Front. To help conceal that weapon from the Germans before it was used against them on the battlefield, British leaders told a series of lies. For example, they said it was a water tank designed to transport water to the front lines, not an armored fighting machine or a "landship," which was the name they used behind closed doors; this is how the tank got its name. They also said that the manufacturing firm building the tanks was not involved in making armaments. Moreover, the British tried to make it appear during the manufacturing process that the tanks were headed for Russia, not the Western Front. Each machine "carried the legend 'With Care to Petrograd' in Russian letters 12 inches high."[14]

This same logic was also at play in Moscow's handling of its biological weapons during the last fifteen years of the Cold War.[15] Despite signing the Biological and Toxins Weapons Convention, which went into effect in March 1975, the Soviets violated that treaty by developing a massive biological weapons program. They did not simply conceal the program from the outside world, but lied about it as well.

Moscow's lying was most prominently on display in 1979, after about one hundred people died near Sverdlovsk after becoming infected with anthrax accidentally released from a biological weapons facility. The Soviets, hoping to avoid getting caught violating the convention, falsely claimed that the deaths were caused by contaminated meat. The ultimate goal in this case and the others described here is to surreptitiously gain and maintain a military advantage over rival states.

Third, a country's leaders might downplay their hostile intentions toward another state to disguise an attack on it. Probably the best example of this phenomenon is Hitler's efforts between 1933 and 1938 to convince the other European powers that he was committed to peace, when he was actually bent on war. "If it rests with Germany," he said in August 1934, "war will not come again. This country has a more profound impression than any other of the evil that war causes.... In our belief Germany's present-day problems cannot be settled by war."[16] And in a famous speech in the Berlin Sportpalast during the tension filled days just before the infamous Munich agreement was signed, he boldly stated that his desire to acquire the Sudetenland for Germany "is the last territorial claim which I will have to make in Europe."[17] Both statements were obvious lies.

Another example of this kind of behavior involves Japan and the Soviet Union in the last year of World War II. They had a neutrality pact throughout most of World War II, but at Yalta in February 1945, Stalin promised Churchill and Roosevelt that the Red Army would attack Japan within three months after Nazi Germany was defeated. Japanese leaders suspected that such a deal had been made at Yalta and queried their Soviet counterparts, who replied that their relationship had not changed at all and was "developing normally on the basis" of the neutrality pact.[18] The Soviets attacked Japan on August 8, 1945.

Sometimes leaders bent on concealing an aggressive action against another country are forced to lie about it when reporters at home start asking probing questions about the impending operation. Those lies, however, are ultimately aimed at the country that is being targeted, not the leaders' own citizens. During the 1960 presidential campaign, for example, John F. Kennedy—the Democratic Party's candidate—argued that the United States should help anti-Castro forces overthrow the Cuban leader.[19] His opponent, Vice President Richard Nixon, knew that the government was deeply involved in just such a scheme. But he also understood that he ran the risk of exposing the operation if he agreed with Kennedy. So he lambasted his opponent's proposal—calling it "probably the most dangerously irresponsible recommendation that he's made during the course of the campaign"—even though he thought it was a smart idea and had fought for that policy inside the government. Nixon was lying to deceive Castro, not the American people. Indeed, he only wished he could tell them the truth.

President Jimmy Carter's press secretary, Jody Powell, was put in a similar situation in April 1980, when a reporter asked him whether it was true that the United States was planning to launch a military operation to free the American hostages then being held in Iran. Although it was true, Powell felt that he had no choice but to lie and say it was not true, because otherwise he would have tipped off the Iranian government about the forthcoming rescue attempt.[20] So he reluctantly deceived the reporter.

Fourth, a state might lie to downplay its hostile intentions toward a rival state, not to facilitate an attack, but to avoid needlessly provoking that rival. This logic was in evidence during the early days of the Cold War, when the countries of Western Europe created two mutual defense pacts: the Treaty of Dunkirk (1947) and the Treaty of Brussels (1948).

Both agreements were said to be checks against a resurgent Germany, but in fact they were mainly designed to contain Soviet expansion in Europe. British and French leaders lied about the real purpose of these alliances because they did not want to antagonize the Soviet Union—which they saw as a serious threat—if they could avoid it.[21]

A fifth kind of inter-state lying is when a country attempts to affect the behavior of a rival state by threatening to attack it, even though it has no intention of actually starting a war. That empty threat might be designed to coerce an adversary into doing something it does not want to do. Germany's behavior during the 1905–6 Moroccan Crisis is an instance of this kind of bluffing. German policymakers were determined to provoke a crisis with France over Morocco that would cause the breakup of the recently formed *entente cordiale* between Britain and France. They threatened war in pursuit of that goal, although "at no stage of the Moroccan affair," as the historian Norman Rich writes, "was a military solution ever advocated or seriously contemplated by the German leaders."[22]

This empty-threat strategy can also be employed to deter an adversary from pursuing a particular policy. For example, in August 1986 the Reagan administration was worried that Libyan leader Muammar al-Gaddafi might be planning to initiate a major terrorist campaign. To prevent that from happening, the White House put out false reports that Gaddafi "was about to be attacked again by U.S. bombers and perhaps be ousted in a coup."[23] Although the United States had no intention of bombing Libya, it hoped that Gaddafi would think that the threat was credible and abandon any plans he might have to support terrorism.

NATO's nuclear policy during the Cold War is another case of an empty threat being used for deterrence purposes. The alliance's official position was that if the Warsaw Pact nations attacked Western Europe and began advancing across Germany, NATO would employ its nuclear weapons to force the Soviet Union and its allies to halt their offensive and possibly even retreat back to their starting positions along the intra-German border. However, some important American policymakers, including former secretary of state Henry Kissinger and former secretary of defense Robert McNamara, publicly endorsed this policy when they were in office, but later made clear that they would not have used nuclear weapons to defend Western Europe in the event of a massive Soviet conventional attack.[24] Their unwillingness to initiate nuclear war was largely a result of the fact that Moscow would surely have retaliated against the United States with its own nuclear weapons, thus risking mutual suicide. Still, it made good sense for NATO policymakers to tell the Soviets that the alliance would use its nuclear weapons to defend Western Europe, even if they thought that was a crazy idea, because Moscow could never be sure that those weapons would not be used, which significantly enhanced deterrence.

Sixth, leaders might lie to provoke another state into attacking their state or another country. Bismarck's behavior in the run-up to the Franco-Prussian War (1870) is probably the most well-known case of a leader purposely giving another country a *casus belli* to attack his own state.[25] And he did it with the help of well-told lies. The Prussian chancellor was committed to creating a unified Germany, and he believed that provoking France to declare war against Prussia, or even a major crisis that threw France into a state of turmoil, would help achieve that goal. Toward that end, he began working assiduously in the spring of 1870 to put a Prussian prince on the throne of Spain, knowing full well that it would alarm and anger France. He denied, however, that he had anything to do with that ploy, which was a lie.

Bismarck spread a second and more important falsehood when he "doctored" the famous Ems Dispatch from Kaiser Wilhelm I to Napoleon III. After the chancellor's efforts to place a Prussian noble on the Spanish throne failed, the French demanded that the kaiser promise that he would not raise the issue again. In his draft response, the kaiser said no, but he left the door open for further negotiations. Fearing that this might lead to a peaceful resolution of the crisis, Bismarck edited the kaiser's draft to make it look like the kaiser was not only saying no, but was also closing the door on any further discussion of the matter. The doctored telegram was then published, and there was outrage across France. Shortly thereafter, Napoleon III foolishly declared war against Prussia.

Seventh, a country that is worried that its allies are not paying enough attention to a dangerous rival state might lie about that adversary's capabilities or behavior to make it look more menacing to its allies. The Bush administration engaged in this kind of lying in early 2005, when it was worried that China, Japan, and South Korea did not fully appreciate the seriousness of the threat posed by North Korea.[26] To get their attention, officials from the National Security Council went to Asia and made the case that North Korea had sold Libya uranium hexafluoride, a critical ingredient for making nuclear weapons. But that was not true. Pakistan, not North Korea, had actually sold the uranium hexafluoride to Libya, and although it is possible that Pakistan originally got that compound from North Korea, there is no evidence in the public record that Pyongyang gave it to Islamabad with the understanding that it would eventually be transferred to Libya. In fact, the available evidence indicates that they were separate deals.

An eighth kind of inter-state lie is where leaders mislead to facilitate spying or sabotage during peacetime, as well as to limit the international fallout if caught in the act. For example, the United States engaged in lying after the U-2 spy plane piloted by Gary Powers was shot down over the Soviet Union in the spring of 1960. At the time, President Eisenhower was about to go to Paris to enter into serious negotiations with Premier Khrushchev over a nuclear-test-ban treaty, and he had made it clear that he did not want any complications from the controversial U-2 flights. After the spy plane was brought down, the president was told that the U-2s had a self-destruct mechanism, which guaranteed that neither Powers nor the plane would survive. So after Khrushchev announced the downing of the U-2, the Eisenhower administration declared that it was not a spy plane but a NASA weather-research plane that had accidentally wandered into Soviet airspace. When the Soviets then produced Powers, the State Department said that he had probably lost consciousness from a lack of oxygen and drifted into Soviet airspace. Finally, Washington was forced to admit that Powers was on a spying mission over Soviet territory.

But that was not the end of the lying. The Eisenhower administration then put out the story that although the president approved of the surveillance program, he was not personally involved in the planning of the overflights. In fact, Eisenhower later admitted that "each series of intrusions was planned and executed with my knowledge and permission."[27]

The infamous Lavon affair involving Israel provides another good example of this type of inter-state lying. In 1954, Israel set out to damage Egypt's relations with Britain and the United States by setting up a spy ring inside Egypt that would sabotage American and British facilities, but make it look like the Egyptians were responsible. After bombing the U.S. Information Service libraries in Alexandria and Cairo as well as a few other targets, plans went awry and the saboteurs were caught. Not surprisingly, Israeli Prime Minister Moshe Sharett maintained that it was all a "wicked plot hatched in Alexandria," indeed a "show trial which is being organized there against a group of Jews who have fallen victims to false accusations."[28]

Ninth, states lie to gain advantage in the course of conducting military operations in wartime. During World War II, for example, the British mounted a massive deception campaign against Nazi Germany in which lying was commonplace. Indeed, it was in the context of these operations that Churchill made his famous statement that "in war-time, truth is so precious that she should always be attended by a bodyguard of lies."[29] The British were hardly an exception in this regard, as Roosevelt made clear when he said in May 1942 that he was "perfectly willing to mislead and tell untruths if it will help win the war."[30] In fact, all of the participants in World War II mounted strategic deception campaigns against their rivals. Moreover, this stratagem is employed in virtually every war.[31]

The tenth kind of inter-state lying involves leaders attempting to get a better deal for their country when they are negotiating treaties and other formal agreements. They might lie to their bargaining partners about their own assets or capabilities, or, more likely, they might bluff about their reservation price—the price above or below which they would not be willing to cut a deal. One would expect to find examples of this kind of lying in a wide variety of circumstances, including arms-control and war-termination negotiations on the security side and international debt, trade, and monetary dealings on the economic side. After all, that is what happens when individuals negotiate over the selling price of a car or a house. Moreover, bargaining theory, which has attracted much attention among international-relations scholars in recent years, would seem to predict a good deal of lying in these circumstances. "Bargaining power," in the words of Nobel Prize–winning economist Thomas Schelling, is "the power to fool and bluff," and bluffing, of course, is all about "the conveyance of false information."[32]

To my surprise, I have only been able to find a few examples of leaders or diplomats lying or bluffing when they are negotiating treaties or other kinds of covenants.[33] There may in fact be many such cases, but if so they have been covered up and are not part of the historical record. But I think not. There is no question that someone who succeeds at bluffing is unlikely to boast about it right after the fact. It makes much more sense to cover up the lie or at least be circumspect about it.[34] Otherwise, the other side might demand to renegotiate the deal or be loath to cut future deals for fear of being played for a sucker again. Still, this line of argument does not make sense because—as I discussed earlier—it is difficult to hide a lie for a long period of time. It is hard to believe that bluffing in international negotiations has been commonplace over time, but very few cases have been revealed to the public.[35]

One case that has been revealed involves Greece lying about its budget deficits so that it could gain entry into the eurozone. [36] According to the European Union's rules, a member country should only be allowed to adopt the euro as its currency if it maintains deficits that are less than 3 percent of the gross domestic product. During the late 1990s, when Greece was being evaluated for possible admission into the eurozone, it was running deficits that were well above that threshold. To deal with this problem, Athens simply lied about the numbers for the relevant years, claiming that its deficits were well under 3 percent when they were not. The gambit worked, and Greece adopted the single currency in 2001.

The United States also lied to its Western European allies (France, Germany, Italy, and the Benelux countries) in the early 1950s to try to persuade them to ratify the European Defense Community (EDC) Treaty, which they had signed in May 1952. The Eisenhower administration strongly supported ratification, in the hope that a functioning EDC could balance the Soviet Union and enable the United States to withdraw most of its troops from Western Europe. As the historian Marc Trachtenberg puts it, "The real point of EDC... was to weld France and Germany together as the core of a strong European federation that could stand up to Russia on its own, and thus make it possible for American forces to withdraw from Europe in the near future."[37]

The Europeans, however, suspected that American support for the EDC was driven largely by Washington's desire to leave the continent, which was an outcome that most Europeans, and especially the French, did not want at all. To deal with this problem, the Eisenhower administration repeatedly assured its allies that ratifying the EDC would not precipitate an American withdrawal, when that was not true. And when there were leaks to the press about what the Americans were up to, Secretary of State John Foster Dulles, as one scholar put it, "was willing to openly lie and state to the press that no U.S. troop withdrawals were being contemplated."[38]

WHEN STATES TELL EACH OTHER LIES

There are four sets of circumstances which are likely to promote inter-state lying, which is not to say that leaders frequently lie in these situations. Countries that are located in dangerous areas where there is intense security competition are more likely to lie than states that live in relatively peaceful regions. This tendency is largely a result of the high premium that states place on survival. States that operate in high-threat environments invariably have an acute sense of vulnerability and thus are strongly inclined to employ any tactic or strategy that might enhance their security. In short, lying comes easy to leaders who think that they live in a Hobbesian world.

Leaders are also more likely to lie in a crisis than during periods of relative calm. A state bent on avoiding war will have powerful incentives to spread falsehoods if doing so will help end the crisis without a fight. On the other hand, a leader determined to turn a crisis into a war will almost certainly lie if he thinks that doing so will help create the conditions for launching and winning the war. None of this is to deny that each side in a crisis will be suspicious of the other's pronouncements, which will make it difficult, although not impossible, to tell persuasive lies.

Furthermore, inter-state lying is likely to be much more prevalent in wartime than peacetime. In his 1928 book on lying during World War I, the British politician Arthur Ponsonby writes that "there must have been more deliberate lying in the world from 1914 to 1918 than in any other period of the world's history."[39] Although it would be virtually impossible to prove that claim because of the impracticality of counting all of the international lies told over time, there surely was a substantial amount of lying during the Great War, as Ponsonby and others make clear. At the same time, it is hard to think of a five-year period during the century before 1914—when few wars were fought in Europe—where there is evidence of lying on the scale we see in World War I.

It is not surprising that leaders often turn to lying when shooting starts. War is a deadly serious business in which foreign-policy elites often think that their states' survival is at stake. But even in conflicts where the stakes are lower—like the United States in Vietnam or the Soviet Union in Afghanistan—leaders usually believe that defeat would do serious damage to their national interest. That kind of thinking makes it easy for leaders to justify lying. There are also many opportunities to lie in wartime, since wars consist of numerous political and military engagements in which there are powerful incentives to deceive the other side. This is why deception is considered an integral part of war.

Finally, leaders are more likely to lie to rival states than allies. "Truth for friends and lies for enemies," as one scholar put it many years ago.[40] By definition, a rival is more dangerous than an ally, which means that it is more important to find ways to gain an advantage over an adversary than a friendly country. Lying sometimes serves that purpose. And because allies can help a state deal with a formidable rival, there are strong incentives for countries to have good relations with their allies and to build a modicum of trust with them, which is hardly served by lying to them. Of course, the fact that allies tend to trust each other more than their rivals makes it somewhat easier for allies to lie to each other than to their rivals, who are naturally more suspicious of their adversaries' pronouncements. Still, lying to an ally comes at a stiff price if it is discovered, as it surely would undermine trust and damage the partnership, which would ultimately hurt the country that told the lie.

This is not to deny that states occasionally conclude that it makes good strategic sense to bamboozle an ally. No two countries always have the same interests—including allies—and it is possible in a crisis that one ally will abandon another or even turn on its partner. Moreover, today's friends can morph into tomorrow's enemy. Remember that the Soviet Union attacked Japan at the end of World War II after falsely promising Tokyo a few months earlier that it had no such intentions. The absence of permanent allies explains why the international system is ultimately a self-help world. This basic logic also explains why Israel lied to the United States during the 1960s about the fact that it was developing nuclear weapons. Israeli leaders have long believed that it is essential to have good relations with the United States. But they obviously felt more strongly that Israel needed its own nuclear deterrent to insure its survival, even if it was necessary to lie to the United States to acquire that capability.

CHAPTER 4

Fearmongering

Fearmongering occurs when a state's leaders see a threat emerging but think that they cannot make the public see the wolf at the door without resorting to a deception campaign. Secretary of State Dean Acheson, who worried that the American people might not fully appreciate the danger posed by the Soviet Union in the late 1940s, argued that it was necessary for American leaders to make their arguments "clearer than truth," because otherwise the public would not support the measures that he thought were necessary to deal with the threat.[1] The aim is not just to deceive the average person in the street, but also to target educated elites, including outside experts who might be inclined to downplay the relevant threat in dangerous ways. Fearmongering campaigns can even be directed at government bureaucrats who might be disposed to soft-pedal a threat that their leaders think is particularly menacing. As distasteful as this behavior might be, leaders do it because they believe that it serves the public interest, not to exploit their fellow citizens for personal gain.

The essence of fearmongering is captured by Kemal Atatürk's famous phrase: "For the people, despite the people."[2]

Leaders engaged in fearmongering might work to create a threat that hardly exists in the public's mind, or more likely, they will exaggerate or "hype" a recognized threat that is not causing much alarm outside of government circles. The ultimate goal could be to build support for a containment policy by getting the public to back increased defense spending, enlist in the military, or support a draft. Threat inflation might also be used to mobilize support for launching a war against a dangerous adversary. Although fearmongering usually occurs in peacetime, it can take place in the midst of a war if leaders feel that their public or their military forces are wavering in their commitment to the fight.

Fearmongering has played an important role in U.S. foreign policy over the past seventy years. Indeed, three administrations have employed that strategy in hopes of dragging a reluctant American public into war. As noted, Franklin Roosevelt lied about the USS *Greer* incident in the late summer of 1941 to mobilize public opinion against Germany and hopefully get the United States into World War II.[3] The USS *Greer*, an American destroyer operating in the North Atlantic, joined up with a British military aircraft that was pursuing a German submarine. The plane eventually dropped depth charges, but then had to return to its base because it was running low on fuel. The *Greer*, however, continued to pursue the submarine, which had not been disabled by the British plane's depth charges. The submarine then fired a torpedo at the *Greer*, which responded with its own depth charges. Neither side hit its target. There was a final engagement between the *Greer* and the German submarine a few hours later, but again neither side hit the other.

A week later President Roosevelt went on radio and told the American people three lies about the *Greer* incident. He clearly implied that the attack on the *Greer* was unprovoked. He did not mention the British aircraft, much less that the *Greer* was pursuing the German submarine in tandem with that plane, which dropped depth charges against the submarine before it fired on the *Greer*.[4] Instead, he simply said that the German submarine "fired first upon this American destroyer without warning, and with deliberate design to sink her" in American "defensive waters." This attack, he said, was "piracy—piracy legally and morally."[5]

Furthermore, Roosevelt maintained that the *Greer*'s identity as an American ship was "unmistakable" to the German submarine. In fact, Navy officials had told Roosevelt two days earlier that there was "no positive evidence that [the] submarine knew [the] nationality of [the] ship at which it was firing." Finally, Roosevelt proclaimed that, "We have sought no shooting war with Hitler. We do not seek it now." In fact, he met Churchill the previous month (August), and according to the British prime minister, Roosevelt "said that he would wage war, but not declare it, and that he would become more and more provocative....Everything was to be done to force an 'incident.'... The President...made it clear that he would look for an 'incident' which would justify him in opening hostilities." The *Greer* obviously provided the requisite incident, although it did not lead to American entry into World War II. The Japanese attack at Pearl Harbor on December 7, 1941, coupled with Hitler's declaration of war against the United States four days later, made that happen.

The behavior of President Lyndon Johnson and his principal foreign policy advisors during the infamous Gulf of Tonkin incident in early August 1964 is strikingly similar to Roosevelt's conduct in the *Greer* incident.[6] The state of affairs in South Vietnam at the time was going from bad to worse for the United States. Johnson hoped to rescue the situation by significantly escalating the fight against North Vietnam, but he recognized that the American public had little enthusiasm for fighting a major war in Southeast Asia. Thus the president concluded that he needed a mandate from Congress that sanctioned the use of massive and sustained force against North Vietnam. An opportunity to get Congress to back any escalatory steps Johnson might make came on August 4, 1964, when Washington received word that North Vietnamese patrol boats had attacked an American destroyer, the USS *Maddox,* in the Gulf of Tonkin. The president used this incident to ram the Gulf of Tonkin Resolution through Congress on August 7. It effectively gave him carte blanche to wage war against North Vietnam.

The Johnson administration told two lies about what happened in the waters off the coast of North Vietnam. First, the President and his aides purposely gave the impression that there was no doubt that the August 4 attack had actually taken place. Johnson, for example, responded on August 7 to an official protest from the Soviet leader Khrushchev by saying that there was "complete and incontrovertible evidence" that the North Vietnamese had attacked the *Maddox*.[7] Secretary of Defense Robert McNamara told Senator Bourke Hickenlooper (R-IA) on August 4 that "the evidence was absolutely clear on the attack."[8] The proposed resolution that the administration sent to Capitol Hill on August 5 confidently stated that the North Vietnamese had "deliberately and repeatedly attacked United States naval vessels."[9]

In fact, within hours of the reported attack, the commander of the *Maddox* was reporting that there were good reasons to question whether there actually had been an attack.[10] On August 4, according to historian Fredrik Logevall, Johnson put pressure on McNamara "to find verification of the...incident," surely because he knew that there were doubts about whether the attack had ever occurred.[11]

The following morning, the president's national security advisor, McGeorge Bundy, told his staff that "the amount of evidence we have today is less than we had yesterday."[12] The next day (August 6), Bundy's deputy, Walt Rostow, told a luncheon at the State Department that "it seemed unlikely that there had actually been an attack on... August 4."[13] When Bundy heard about Rostow's remarks, he said that his deputy should be told to "button his lip."[14] In short, it was a falsehood to say or even imply that the United States had no doubts about whether the Maddox had been attacked on August 4.

The second lie concerns the Johnson administration's claim that the Maddox was on a "routine patrol" in the Gulf of Tonkin and that the alleged attack was "deliberate and unprovoked."[15] In fact, one reason that the Maddox was in those waters was to collect intelligence in support of South Vietnamese forces that were attacking the North Vietnamese coast at the time, and, not surprisingly, almost every top-level American policymaker understood that Hanoi would view the Maddox as a party to those attacks.[16] Although the evidence is not air tight, a plausible case can be made that the United States was trying to provoke the North Vietnamese to strike the Maddox.[17] Regardless, Robert McNamara was clearly lying when he told the Senate on August 4: "Our navy played absolutely no part in, was not associated with, was not aware of, any South Vietnamese actions, if there were any.... I say this flatly. This is a fact."[18]

The Bush administration engaged in fearmongering before the United States attacked Iraq on March 19, 2003. There is no question that the president and his principal advisors sincerely believed that Saddam Hussein was a dangerous threat who had to be removed from office sooner rather than later. At the same time, they understood that there was not much enthusiasm for invading Iraq in the broader public. Moreover, the American military, the intelligence community, the State Department, and the U.S. Congress were not keen for war. To overcome this reluctance to attack Iraq, the Bush administration engaged in a deception campaign to inflate the threat posed by Saddam. It involved spinning, concealing, and lying to the American people. I will describe four key lies.

First, Secretary of Defense Donald Rumsfeld said on September 27, 2002 that he had "bulletproof" evidence that Saddam was closely allied with Osama bin Laden.[19] In fact, he had no such evidence, which he admitted on October 4, 2004, when he told the Council on Foreign Relations, "To my knowledge, I have not seen any strong, hard evidence that links the two."[20] Similarly, Secretary of State Colin Powell, who claimed before the war that bin Laden was in "partnership with Iraq" and that there was a "sinister nexus between Iraq and the Al Qaeda terrorist network," admitted in January 2004: "I have not seen smoking-gun, concrete evidence about the connection, but I think the possibility of such connections did exist and it was prudent to consider them at the time that we did."[21]

The Bush administration actually had solid evidence before the war that Saddam and bin Laden were not working together. As noted, two high-level Al Qaeda operatives captured after September 11 independently told their interrogators that there was no link between the two. Moreover, neither the CIA nor the Defense Intelligence Agency (DIA) could find conclusive evidence of a meaningful link between bin Laden and Saddam before the United States invaded Iraq.[22] Nor was the 9/11 Commission able to uncover evidence of a "collaborative relationship" between those two leaders.[23]

Second, the architects of the war often claimed that the United States knew with absolute certainty that Iraq had particular WMD capabilities, when, in fact, that was not true.

There were, of course, good reasons to suspect that Saddam might have chemical and biological weapons, but there was no direct evidence that he possessed those capabilities. Indeed, when Rumsfeld and General Tommy Franks briefed Bush on September 6, 2002, Franks said, "Mr. President, we've been looking for Scud missiles and other weapons of mass destruction for ten years and haven't found any yet, so I can't tell you that I know that there are any specific weapons anywhere. I haven't seen Scud one."[24] Nor did the intelligence agencies have hard evidence that Iraq possessed WMD.[25] Moreover, the UN weapons inspectors were unable to find any evidence of WMD between November 2002 and March 2003, despite having the freedom to look anywhere they wanted inside Iraq. And, of course, if the U.S. government knew where those weapons were, they could have alerted the UN inspectors and helped them find the WMD.

Despite this lack of hard evidence, Vice President Cheney told the Veterans of Foreign Wars in late August 2002 that "there is no doubt that Saddam Hussein now has weapons of mass destruction. There is no doubt that he is amassing them to use against our friends, against our allies, and against us."[26] Secretary of State Powell said one month later that "there is no doubt he has chemical weapons stocks."[27] On February 5, 2003, he told the UN, "There can be no doubt that Saddam Hussein has biological weapons and the capability to produce more, many more."[28] Following suit, President Bush said on March 17, 2003:"Intelligence gathered by this and other governments leaves no doubt that the Iraq regime continues to possess and conceal some of the most lethal weapons ever devised."[29] That same month, Secretary Rumsfeld went even further by saying that the United States knew Saddam had WMD because "we know where they are."[30]

Another example of this line of deception was Vice President Cheney's claim on September 8, 2002 that "we do know, with absolute certainty, that he [Saddam] is using his procurement system to acquire the equipment he needs in order to enrich uranium to build a nuclear weapon."[31] The equipment that Cheney was referring to was the widely discussed aluminum tubes that Iraq had procured from abroad. However, there was sharp disagreement within the intelligence community about the ultimate purpose of those tubes. Some analysts argued that they were designed for centrifuges that would help make nuclear weapons. But others, including experts in the Department of Energy, the agency with the greatest technical expertise on the subject, believed (correctly) that they were designed for artillery rockets.[32] More generally, there were serious doubts within the intelligence community about whether Saddam had reconstituted his nuclear weapons program.[33] In short, we did not know with "absolute certainty" that Iraq was trying to procure aluminum tubes to enrich uranium.

Third, the Bush administration made numerous statements before the war that were designed to imply that Saddam was in part responsible for the attacks on September 11. But the president and his advisors never explicitly said that he was linked to those events. The aim, of course, was to lead the American public to draw a false conclusion about Saddam without plainly stating that conclusion. It is no accident that when the war began in mid-March 2003, about half of the American people believed that the Iraqi dictator had helped bring down the World Trade Center.[34] There is no evidence, however, that Saddam was involved in the September 11 attacks, as President Bush, Vice President Cheney, National Security Advisor Condoleezza Rice, Secretary Rumsfeld, and Deputy Defense Secretary Paul Wolfowitz have all admitted when directly confronted on the matter.[35]

That evidence notwithstanding, the administration went to great lengths to foster that false connection in the minds of the American people. For example, when Senator Mark Dayton (D-MN) asked Rumsfeld on September 19, 2002 to explain what was "compelling us now to make a precipitous decision and take precipitous action" against Iraq when the United States did not feel compelled to do so earlier, the secretary of defense replied, "What's different?—what's different is 3,000 people were killed....What's new is the nexus between terrorist networks like al Qaeda and terrorist states like Iraq."[36] In his March 18, 2003, letter to Congress laying out the justification for invading Iraq, President Bush wrote that the United States was within its legal rights "to take the necessary actions against international terrorists and terrorist organizations, including those nations, organizations, or persons whom planned, authorized, committed, or aided the terrorist attacks that occurred on September 11, 2001."[37]

Even after Baghdad fell in April 2003, Bush and his lieutenants continued to imply that the war in Iraq was directly linked to September 11. For example, when the president spoke on the deck of the USS *Abraham Lincoln* on May 1, 2003, he told his audience, "The battle of Iraq is one victory in a war on terror that began on September the 11th, 2001 and still goes on." He went on to say, "The liberation of Iraq is a crucial advance in the campaign against terror. We have removed an ally of Al Qaida and cut off a source of terrorist funding....We have not forgotten the victims of September the 11th, the last phone calls, the cold murder of children, the searches in the rubble. With those attacks, the terrorists and their supporters declared war on the United States, and war is what they got."[38]

Vice President Cheney, who has also played a key role in spreading this falsehood, said on September 14, 2003, that if the United States prevails in Iraq, "We will have struck a major blow right at the heart of the base, if you will, the geographic base of the terrorists who have had us under assault now for many years, but most especially on 9/11."[39] Again, there is no evidence that Saddam was in cahoots with bin Laden, much less that the Iraqi dictator helped Al Qaeda in any way on September 11. The Bush administration was undoubtedly still pedaling this bogus story to sustain support for the Iraq war, which had begun to go badly in the late summer of 2003.[40]

Fourth, in the year before the war, President Bush and his advisors frequently said that they hoped to find a peaceful resolution to the Iraq crisis, and that war was an option of last resort. For example, Bush told Italian prime minister Silvio Berlusconi on January 30, 2003, that he had not made a decision on whether to use force against Iraq, and then told the American people, with Berlusconi at his side, that it was still possible to avert war, although time was running short.[41] The following week in Munich, Rumsfeld said publicly, "We still hope that force may not be necessary to disarm Saddam Hussein.... Let me be clear: No one wants war."[42]

In fact, the Bush administration was bent on war by the summer of 2002, if not earlier, and the decision to deal with Saddam by going to the UN in September 2002 was designed to provide diplomatic cover, not to avoid the war. For example, Richard Haass, the head of policy planning in the State Department, says he knew that war was inevitable after meeting with Condoleezza Rice in early July 2002. He asked the national security advisor whether it made sense "to put Iraq front and center at this point, given the war on terrorism and other issues. And she said, essentially, that that decision's been made, don't waste your breath."[43]

At roughly the same time, British policymakers concluded that Washington was bent on war against Iraq. Their thinking is summarized in a summary of a meeting chaired by Prime Minister Tony Blair on July 23, 2002. It reads: "C [the head of Britain's Secret Intelligence Service] reported on his recent talks in Washington. There was a perceptible shift in attitude. Military action was now seen as inevitable. Bush wanted to remove Saddam, through military action, justified by the conjunction of terrorism and WMD." It went on to say: "The Foreign Secretary said he would discuss this with Colin Powell this week. It seemed clear that Bush had made up his mind to take military action, even if the timing was not yet decided."[44] Finally, Bush met with Colin Powell on January 13, 2003 and told him that he had decided to go to war against Iraq.[45] That meeting took place a few weeks before Bush told the American public and Berlusconi that it might still be possible to avoid using force against Saddam and a few weeks before Rumsfeld told a Munich audience that war was not inevitable.[46]

WHY LEADERS FEARMONGER

Leaders engage in fearmongering when they think they recognize a serious threat to national security that the public does not see, and that the public cannot be made to appreciate with straightforward and honest discourse.[47] They reason that the only way to mobilize their citizens to do the right thing is to deceive them for their own good. Fearmongering, which is a straightforward top-down form of behavior, is antidemocratic at its core, although leaders do it because they think it is in the national interest, not for personal gain.

There are a number of reasons why average citizens might not be able to comprehend a particular threat. They might not be sufficiently interested in international affairs to appreciate that their country is facing a lurking danger, even when their leaders give them unvarnished evidence of the threat. Moreover, they might not be collectively smart enough to recognize a specific threat. It is also possible that those citizens might get weak-kneed when confronted with a menacing threat. In short, the broader public might be prone to some combination of ignorance, stupidity, and cowardice. When that happens, according to this logic, the governing elites have to light a fire under their people so that they will rise up to meet the challenge.

A good example of this kind of thinking in action was the way the Truman administration attempted to sell a major increase in defense spending to the American people in the spring of 1950.[48] The president and his senior foreign-policy advisors believed that the broader public would not fully support the proposed buildup, and therefore it would be necessary to initiate a "psychological scare campaign." Of course, when policymakers take a country down this road, they will inevitably face pressure to tell lies to scare their people enough that they enthusiastically back the government's planned policies.

It is much harder to argue that educated elites who dispute the seriousness of a threat are either ignorant or dim-witted. This is especially true when you are dealing with experts on the issue at hand. It might be the case, however, that those educated and interested dissenters are perceived to have a wishy-washy view of international politics, and therefore some threat inflation is necessary to stiffen their backbones. It might also be the case that they are simply misreading the available evidence about the danger facing their country and drawing overly optimistic conclusions about the threat environment. If leaders cannot solve this problem by providing the misguided dissenters with more detailed information, the only solution left is fearmongering.

Bamboozling those recalcitrant elites is unlikely to work, however, because those dissenters are by definition knowledgeable about the issue at hand and thus hard to fool. An alternative approach, which is more likely to work, is to use fearmongering to mobilize the broader public in ways that make it suspicious, if not hostile, to those stubborn experts. They would then be isolated and feel suspect, and maybe even worried about their careers, which would make them more likely to temper their criticisms or remain silent, or maybe even shift gears and support the government's policy. Leslie Gelb, the former president of the Council on Foreign Relations, candidly acknowledged that this kind of fear caused him to support the 2003 Iraq war: "My initial support for the war was symptomatic of unfortunate tendencies within the foreign policy community, namely the disposition and incentives to support wars to retain political and professional credibility."[49]

There is an alternative explanation for why leaders sometimes turn to fearmongering that is less contemptuous of the public. It is possible that a country's political system might be prone to paralysis and thus unable to respond in a timely manner to a serious threat. The fledgling American government under the Articles of Confederation certainly fits this description, and some even argue that the system of checks and balances set up under the Constitution is not conducive to recognizing and dealing with external threats in a timely manner.[50] Leaders will have powerful incentives to fearmonger when the governmental machinery is sclerotic, because rousing the people might be the only way to force the political system into action to meet the looming danger.

It is reasonably easy for policymakers to lie to their publics. For starters, they control the state's intelligence apparatus, which gives them access to important information that the public does not have and cannot get, at least in the short term. Policymakers, therefore, can manipulate the flow of information to the public in various ways, and most people will be inclined to trust what their leaders tell them unless there is hard evidence that they are being deceived.

Furthermore, the head of a country can use the bully pulpit to manipulate the discourse about foreign policy in different ways, including lying to the public. American presidents have significant power in this regard.

Lying to the public is relatively easy for another reason. As noted, it is difficult for statesmen to lie to each other about significant matters, because there is not much trust between countries. Anarchy pushes states to be vigilant in their dealings with each other, especially when national security issues are at play. But that is not the case inside most states, where large numbers of people, including educated elites, are predisposed to trust their government, whose most important job, after all, is to protect them. Robert McNamara once said that it is "inconceivable that anyone even remotely familiar with our society and system of government could suspect the existence of a conspiracy" to provoke a war.[51] Many Americans would readily endorse McNamara's claim, as they expect their leaders to be straight with them. This trust, of course, is what makes the public easy to fool, and this is why the behavior that McNamara describes is not just thinkable, but we have evidence of it.

One might surmise that fearmongering does not pay because the liar will eventually get caught and be punished by his public. He might lose credibility with his citizens or maybe even be voted out of office when he comes up for reelection. These possibilities are not much of a deterrent, however, mainly because leaders who lie to their publics think they can get away with it. For starters, it is not clear that the lies will be unmasked anytime soon. It took more than thirty years before it became public knowledge that President Kennedy had lied about how he settled the Cuban missile crisis. As discussed in the next chapter, he agreed to a secret deal with the Soviets in which the United States would remove its Jupiter missiles from Turkey in exchange for the Soviets taking their missiles out of Cuba. But Kennedy and his advisors denied making that deal during and after the crisis.

Furthermore, perpetrators are likely to think that even if they get caught, they will be able to rely on smart lawyers and friends in high places to help them craft a clever defense so that they can escape punishment. Finally, and most importantly, leaders who engage in fearmongering invariably believe that their assessment of the threat is correct, even if they are lying about some of the particulars. They think that they are in the right and what they are doing is for the good of the country. Thus, their lies will matter little in the long run if they expose the threat for what it is and deal with it effectively. The end result, in other words, will justify the means.

This line of thinking surely underpinned the Bush administration's deception campaign in the run-up to the war in Iraq, and it probably would have worked if the United States had won a stunning victory, like it did in the 1991 war against Iraq. A comment by *Washington Post* columnist Richard Cohen in November 2005, when the second Iraq war was going badly, illustrates the cleansing power of military victory: "One could almost forgive President Bush for waging war under false or mistaken pretenses had a better, more democratic Middle East come out of it."[52]

WHEN ELITES ARE LIKELY TO FEARMONGER

Regime type influences the likelihood of fearmongering. In particular, it is more likely in democracies than autocracies, because leaders are more beholden to public opinion in democratic states. Of course, not all democratically elected leaders will surmise that their people need to be deceived because they cannot assess the facts of a situation correctly or handle the truth; but some will. There is actually a rich tradition of this kind of thinking on the right in America, where it is widely believed that democracies are at a disadvantage when they compete against nondemocracies, because the broader public is an obstacle to developing a smart and bold foreign policy. This line of thinking was evident during the Cold War, especially among neoconservatives and other hardliners like James Burnham and Jean-François Revel, who thought that the publics in the democratic West were prone to appease rather than confront their dangerous adversaries.[53]

Neoconservative thinking about the broader public's inability to handle truth is captured in the following comment by Irving Kristol, one of the founding fathers of that movement: "There are different kinds of truth for different kinds of people. There are truths appropriate for children; truths that are appropriate for students; truths that are appropriate for educated adults; and truths that are appropriate for highly educated adults, and the notion that there should be one set of truths available to everyone is a modern democratic fallacy. It doesn't work."[54] This perspective, however, is not restricted to conservatives, as is evident from reading *The Phantom Public* by Walter Lippmann, who was not a man of the right.[55]

This kind of behavior may be more prevalent in democracies, but it is not limited to them, because in the age of nationalism, even the leaders of nondemocratic countries pay attention to public opinion. Hitler, for example, closely monitored the German people's thinking about all kinds of issues, and went to great lengths to ensure that his policies enjoyed widespread public support. His regime, as Ian Kershaw reminds us, was "acutely aware of the need to manufacture consensus."[56] Nevertheless, the more autocratic or the more firm the autocrat's grip on his society, the less likely the need for fearmongering.

Geography also influences the likelihood of fearmonger-ing. States that share a border with a menacing adversary usu-ally have little need to exaggerate that threat, mainly because it resides next door and is in easy striking distance. In such cases, the public is likely to recognize and fear its next-door neighbor. On the other hand, countries that do not share a border with a dangerous opponent are more likely to have cause to rely on fearmongering. A distant enemy is likely to appear less frightening than a nearby enemy and thus give leaders reason to inflate the threat. States separated from their main adversaries and allies by large bodies of water—I call these states offshore balancers—are especially prone to fearmongering, because water is a formidable defensive barrier.[57]

Comparing the amount of threat inflation in each of the major powers during World War I illustrates how geography influences the rhetoric that leaders employ to describe their adversaries. There was much less fearmongering about the German threat in France and Russia than there was in Brit-ain and the United States. This is hardly surprising, since the two Anglo-Saxon countries are offshore balancers; in con-trast, France and Russia not only shared a border with the *Kaiserreich,* but they were also fighting the German army on their own territory. Germany itself had little need to threat-inflate during the war, since it was fighting against adversar-ies located on both its eastern and western borders.

Finally, leaders promoting wars of choice—especially *preventive wars*—are likely to engage in fearmongering. It is difficult to motivate the public to support a preventive war, which is when one country attacks another that is not an imminent threat to it at that time, but might be sometime in the future. Because the threat is not serious at the moment, the public's sense of danger is unlikely to be high. Moreover, given the difficulty of predicting the future, many citizens are likely to think that the threat might not ever materialize for one reason or another. Preventive wars are also prohibited by international law as well as just-war theory, which make them a hard sell in many countries around the world. For these reasons, many people—including experts—will want to adopt a "wait and see" policy, and hope that trouble never shows up. To counter this foot dragging, the advocates of war will fearmonger to create the impression that the country is facing an immediate threat and that they are advocating *preemptive war,* which is when a country attacks an adversary that is about to attack it. Preemptive wars, which are essentially a form of self-defense, are widely recognized as legal as well as just.[58]

Regarding the run-up to the current war in Iraq, it is worth noting that the United States is a democracy as well as an offshore balancer, and it was attempting to sell a preventive war. Not surprisingly, the Bush administration told lies and engaged in other kinds of deception to create the impression that Saddam was an imminent threat and that the United States would thus be fighting a preemptive war, not a preventive war.[59]

CHAPTER 5

Strategic Cover-ups

Strategic cover-ups can take two forms. Leaders can lie about a policy that has gone badly wrong. The motivating reason for the falsehood is to protect the country's interests, not to shield the individuals who are responsible for the policy failure, although that is usually an unintended consequence. Leaders can also lie to hide a controversial but smart strategy, because they fear that it will meet serious public resistance and not be adopted. The aim in this instance is not to conceal a bungled policy from the body politic, but to implement a particular policy without arousing strong opposition. In both cases, however, the leaders believe that there are sound strategic reasons for the cover-up. They are lying for what they judge to be the good of the country.

Inter-state lies are directed at other states, while fearmongering is directed at the home front. Strategic cover-ups, in contrast, are usually aimed at both of those audiences. To be more specific, a leader bent on covering up a controversial or failed policy will always seek to deceive his public and will frequently try to deceive another country at the same time. In other words, the intended audience for a strategic cover-up can either be the home front alone or the home front plus a foreign audience. But the target of this kind of falsehood cannot be just another country, because that would be an inter-state lie.

Strategic cover-ups, it should be emphasized, are not examples of concealment, which is when leaders deceive their intended audience by hardly saying anything about an important foreign policy problem. With strategic cover-ups, leaders are dealing with international issues that have a public face and are certain to prompt hard questions that the government will have to answer. In those cases, however, leaders will tell lies because they believe that it is in the national interest to deceive their fellow citizens, and often other states as well.

WHY LEADERS ENGAGE IN STRATEGIC COVER-UPS

One reason that leaders sometimes seek to hide failure and the incompetence that caused it is because they do not want to convey weakness to an adversary who might exploit it, or because they think that it might damage their relationship with other countries. Of course, they also worry about the home front, where news about botched operations and ineptitude can undermine national unity, which is especially important when fighting a protracted war that is not going well.

During World War I, for example, Marshal Joseph Joffre, the commander-in-chief of the French army, bungled the planning for the battle of Verdun (1916) and then mismanaged the battle itself. He was clearly incompetent and most French political leaders knew it. But they could not tell the public that he was inept when thousands of French soldiers under his command were being wounded or killed each week. They feared that revealing the true facts about Joffre would badly weaken morale on the home front and possibly undermine the war effort. So the politicians concealed their critical discussions about Joffre from the public and falsely portrayed him as an able leader. "Concern for morale," as the scholar Ian Ousby writes, "prevented him falling into official disgrace."[1] It also would have been foolish to reveal to the Germans that the French forces facing them at Verdun were in serious trouble because they were under the command of an inept general.

Israel's behavior in the aftermath of the infamous Qibya massacre is another case of a state covering up a failed policy for what its leaders felt were good strategic reasons.[2] On October 14, 1953, a commando force headed by Major Ariel Sharon went into the West Bank village of Qibya and murdered sixty-nine Palestinians, roughly two-thirds of whom were women and children. The attack was in retaliation for the killing of an Israeli woman and her two young children a day earlier. The orders from Israel's central command, which oversaw the raid, stipulated that the objective was "attacking the village of Qibya, temporarily occupying it, and maximal killing in order to chase the inhabitants of the village from their houses."[3]

There was a huge outcry around the world—including from the American Jewish community—when it became known what the Israeli commandos had done in Qibya. Oxford scholar Avi Shlaim writes that "The Qibya massacre unleashed against Israel a storm of international protest of unprecedented severity in the country's short history."[4] News about the raid was also causing problems for the Israeli government on the home front.[5] Fully aware of the potential for further trouble at home, not to mention the damage that was being done to Israel's international standing, Israeli leaders tried to rescue the situation by lying. "On October 19," Israeli historian Benny Morris writes, Prime Minister David Ben-Gurion "went on the air with a wholly fictitious account of what happened." He blamed the massacre on Jewish frontier settlers and said, "The Government of Israel rejects with all vigor the absurd and fantastic allegation that 600 men of the IDF took part in the action.... We have carried out a searching investigation and it is clear beyond doubt that not a single army unit was absent from its base on the night of the attack on Qibya."[6] But Ben-Gurion's lying did not work, and on November 24 the UN Security Council passed a resolution expressing "the strongest censure of that action."

Leaders might also lie to cover up a controversial policy that they believe is strategically sound, but that they want to hide from their own public and possibly other countries as well. The underlying assumption is that most of their fellow citizens are unlikely to have sufficient wisdom to recognize the policy's virtues. Therefore, it makes sense for the leaders to adopt the policy but conceal that fact from their people; otherwise, public opinion might force the government to abandon the policy, to the country's detriment. The same harsh assessment of the public's ability to think wisely that underpins fearmongering underpins strategic cover-ups.

President John F. Kennedy's efforts to bring the Cuban Missile Crisis to a peaceful conclusion provide a good example of a leader lying to cover up a controversial policy.[7] To end that crisis before it escalated into a war between the superpowers, Kennedy agreed to the Soviet demand that the United States pull its nuclear-armed Jupiter missiles out of Turkey in return for the Soviets pulling their missiles out of Cuba. The president understood that this concession would not play well with the American public, especially with the political right, and would also damage Washington's relations with its NATO allies, especially Turkey. So he told the Soviets that they could not speak openly about the deal, or else he would have to deny it and ultimately renege on it. Still, there were suspicions in the West that such a deal had been cut, and the Kennedy administration was queried on the matter. The president and his principal advisors lied and denied that there had been an agreement to take the Jupiters out of Turkey. In retrospect, it appears to have been a noble lie, since it helped defuse an extremely dangerous confrontation between two states armed with nuclear weapons.

Between 1922 and 1933, the German military trained in the Soviet Union in clear violation of the Versailles Treaty.[8] German leaders were fearful that if these activities were exposed, they would be heavily criticized by Weimar Germany's political left, as well as by Britain and France, who would all push hard to end this valuable but illegal arrangement. Not surprisingly, the German government lied to help conceal it. An even more controversial case occurred in Britain during the mid-1950s, when parliament began to hear stories that the colonial government in Kenya was running a gulag for Mau Mau independence fighters.[9] The British government feared that if this story became widely known, public opinion would force an end to Britain's violent policies in Kenya, which would probably mean victory for the Mau Mau. That precedent, of course, would not bode well for maintaining the larger empire. To deal with these explosive revelations, British leaders lied about the Kenyan gulag and smeared the individuals who tried to expose it.

Finally, we now know that Japan reached a number of secret agreements with the United States during the Cold War. For example, Tokyo agreed in 1969 to allow nuclear-armed American ships to dock at Japanese ports.[10] There was also a secret accord that called for Japan to help pay a large part of the cost of stationing American troops on Japanese soil. These agreements would have been exceedingly controversial had they been made public; in fact, the ensuing uproar probably would have forced Japan's leaders to abrogate them. After all, the law in Japan prohibited nuclear-armed vessels from entering Japanese ports. Because the leadership thought that the accords were in Japan's national interest, they were hidden from the public. However, it did not take long before outsiders began to suspect that those agreements existed, and point blank questions about them were directed at Japanese leaders. Not surprisingly, they responded by lying and denying that those deals had been struck.

WHEN STRATEGIC COVER-UPS ARE LIKELY

Stipulating when strategic cover-ups are more or less likely is somewhat complicated because this kind of deception involves two kinds of behavior—hiding incompetence and masking controversial policies—and two different audiences—other countries and the leader's own public.

For starters, let us focus on the question of when a leader is likely to lie to help hide either a failed or controversial policy from another country. Not surprisingly, the circumstances that are likely to push leaders to engage in inter-state lying also apply to strategic cover-ups. In both cases, leaders are lying to another state because they think it is in the national interest. This means that leaders are more likely to engage in strategic cover-ups aimed at foreign audiences when their country is: (1) located in a dangerous region, (2) involved in a crisis, (3) engaged in a war, or (4) dealing with a rival rather than an ally.

Strategic cover-ups, of course, are more than just inter-state lies; leaders direct them at their own people as well as the outside world. Masking incompetence from the public is most likely to occur in wartime, especially if the conflict is thought to be a fight for survival. The stakes will be so high in such a situation that leaders will not hesitate to lie to their citizenry if they think that it is necessary to avoid defeat and win the war. Furthermore, it is relatively easy to hide mistakes from the public in the midst of a war, because that is a circumstance in which governments are invariably given lots of leeway to limit and manipulate the flow of information. Plus, deception is widely considered to be an important instrument for fighting a deadly adversary. Finally, botched operations of one sort or another are commonplace in almost every conflict, which means that there will be plenty of opportunities, as well as the incentive, to engage in strategic cover-ups.[11]

What about controversial policies? They are more likely to be hidden from the public in democracies than nondemocracies. The most obvious reason for this is that leaders in a democracy must pay more attention to public opinion, because they are held accountable for their actions through regular elections. They cannot enunciate a policy that they think is wise but sure to be unpopular and then ignore the political fallout. In such cases, leaders have powerful incentives to adopt the policy, but not announce the decision publicly, and then lie if necessary to cloak what they have done. There is certainly some accountability in nondemocracies, but usually not as much as in democracies. Therefore, a leader of a nondemocratic state will be less inclined to veil a divisive policy from his public than his counterpart in a democracy.

There are also likely to be more situations that encourage leaders to lie to help conceal a controversial policy in a democracy than a nondemocracy. It is commonplace to have vigorous and contentious public debates about weighty issues in democracies, which means that leaders are almost certain to be asked tough questions about their preferred policies.

There is also a powerful norm of transparency in democracies, which means that leaders are expected to provide serious answers to those questions, which includes providing the public with some reasonable amount of information on the issue at hand. These circumstances make it hard to hide a controversial policy without lying. In contrast, there are usually not big public fights over policies in nondemocracies, which makes it easier for leaders to hide potentially divisive policies without having to lie about them. Thus, when dealing with controversial policies, there is a stronger incentive for democratic leaders to lie than their counterparts in nondemocracies.

The bottom line is that the likelihood that states will cover up a policy debacle or conceal a controversial policy is usually determined by the same set of conditions that influence inter-state lying, but with two important twists: covering up failed policies is especially likely in wartime, and concealing a contentious policy is especially likely in democracies.

CHAPTER 6

Nationalist Myths

With the rise of nationalism over the past two centuries, numerous ethnic or national groups around the world have established or have tried to establish their own state, or what is commonly called a nation-state. In the process, each group has created its own sacred myths about the past that portray it in a favorable way and portray rival national groups in a negative light.[1] MIT political scientist Stephen Van Evera argues that these chauvinist myths "come in three principal varieties: self-glorifying, self-whitewashing, and other-maligning."[2] Inventing these myths and purveying them widely invariably requires lying about the historical record as well as contemporary political events. "Historical error," as the French political theorist Ernest Renan succinctly put it, "is a crucial factor in the creation of a nation."[3]

WHY ELITES CREATE NATIONALIST MYTHS

The elites who dominate a nation's discourse are largely responsible for inventing its myths, and they do so for two main reasons. These false stories help fuel group solidarity; they help create a powerful sense of nationhood, which is essential for building and maintaining a viable nation-state. In particular, these fictions help give members of a national group the sense that they are part of a noble enterprise, which they should not only be proud of, but for which they should be willing to endure significant hardships, including fighting and dying if necessary. This need to accentuate the positive in a nation's past is reflected in a law passed by the French government in February 2005, which mandated that high school history courses and textbooks must henceforth emphasize the positive aspects of French colonialism.[4]

The creation of national myths, however, is not simply a case of elites concocting false stories and transmitting them to their publics. In fact, the common people invariably hunger for these myths; they want to be told stories about the past in which they are portrayed as the white hats and opposing nations as the black hats. In effect, nationalist mythmaking is driven from below as well as from above.

Elites also create national myths to gain international legitimacy.[5] The payoffs on this front are usually small, however, because it is difficult to hoodwink outsiders with stories that are at odds with a fair reading of the historical record. Still, there are two possible exceptions to this rule. Leaders might be able to sell their national myths to a close ally who has a vested interest in accepting those false stories as true. In the wake of World War II, for example, German elites created the myth that their military—the Wehrmacht—had little to do with the mass killings of innocent civilians on the Eastern Front during that brutal war.[6] It was said that the

SS—which represented a much narrower slice of German society and was closely identified with Hitler—was largely responsible for those vast horrors. The Wehrmacht, according to this legend, had "clean hands."

The United States largely bought into this false story during the early years of the Cold War, because it was then working closely with former Nazis, Nazi collaborators, and former members of the Wehrmacht, and also because it was committed to rehabilitating the German army and making it an integral part of NATO. Not surprisingly, as Christopher Simpson notes in his book about Washington's recruitment of Nazis after Word War II, "a review of the more popular histories of the war published in the West during those years, with a few lonely exceptions, leaves the distinct impression that the savageries of the Holocaust were strictly the SS's responsibility, and not all of the SS at that."[7] Beginning in the late 1960s, however, German scholars began to unravel the real story, which was that the Wehrmacht had been an integral part of the German killing machine during World War II. But, by then, the new German military (the Bundeswehr) and NATO were well established, and it was not a serious political problem for the United States to accept the truth about what happened on the Eastern Front between 1939 and 1945.

It is also sometimes feasible for a state with an influential diaspora to export its myths to the countries where the diaspora is located. Perhaps the best example of this phenomenon involves Israel and the American Jewish community. There was no way that the Zionists could create a Jewish state in Palestine without doing large-scale ethnic cleansing of the Arab population that had been living there for centuries. This point was widely recognized by the Zionist leadership well before Israel was created. The opportunity to expel the Palestinians came in early 1948 when fighting broke out between

the Palestinians and the Zionists in the wake of the UN decision to partition Palestine into two states. The Zionists cleansed
roughly 700,000 Palestinians from the land that became Israel,
and adamantly refused to let them return to their homes once
the fighting stopped. Of course, this was a story that cast Israel
in the role of the victimizer and would make it difficult for
the fledgling state to win friends and influence people around
the world, especially in the United States.

Not surprisingly, Israel and its American friends went to
great lengths after the events of 1948 to blame the expul-
sion of the Palestinians on the victims themselves. According to the myth that was invented, the Palestinians were
not cleansed by the Zionists; instead, they were said to have
fled their homes because the surrounding Arab countries
told them to move out so that their armies could move in
and drive the Jews into the sea. The Palestinians could then
return home after the Jews had been cleansed from the land.
This story was widely accepted not only in Israel but also
in the United States for about four decades, and it played
a key role in convincing many Americans to look favor-
ably upon Israel in its ongoing conflict with the Palestinians. Israeli scholars, however, have demolished that myth
and others over the past two decades, and the new history
has slowly begun to affect the discourse in the United States
about the Israeli-Palestinian conflict in ways that make at
least some Americans less sympathetic to Israel's past and
present actions toward the Palestinians.[8]

WHEN ELITES ENGAGE IN NATIONALIST MYTHMAKING

Nations continuously purvey their core myths, because most
individuals in the group need those stories to make sense of
their own identity, and because they foster group solidarity.

So, one could say that nationalist mythmaking happens all the time. Of course, those stories have to be updated from time to time, as new information about the past emerges, and fresh myths have to be created to deal with significant new episodes in the nation's history. Thus, one would expect the telling of nationalist lies to intensify in the wake of wars and other high-profile incidents where there are serious disputes about the behavior of the nation in question, which might even trigger renewed controversy about older disputes which had been quiescent. In such cases, elites will work overtime to portray their nation in the most positive light and rival nations in the harshest possible light.

One would also expect nationalist mythmaking to be especially intense when there are serious disputes about a country's founding. The legitimacy of a state is bound up in important ways with the circumstances surrounding its birth, and most people do not want to think that their country was "born in sin." How much lying takes place in such cases is largely a function of two factors: the level of brutality involved in creating the nation-state, and how recently it happened.

Specifically, the more brutal the state-building process is, the more bad behavior there is to hide, and thus the greater the need for elites to lie about what actually happened when the state was created. Self-whitewashing myths, as Van Evera notes, are probably the most common of his three kinds of nationalist lies.[9] And the more recent the relevant events, the more likely it is that people on different sides of the conflict will remember and care deeply about them. In short, when the founding of a country was recent and cruel, the elites will have to work overtime to fabricate a story that portrays their side as knights in shining armor and the other side as the devil incarnate.

Consider, for example, the fifteen states that emerged from the wreckage of the former Soviet Union. There was little need for the elites in any of those countries to invent false stories about how they came into being in 1991, largely because the breakup of the Soviet Union was remarkably peaceful. (All of those remnant states, of course, have powerful incentives to lie about other aspects of their long histories, and they do.) Contrast that set of cases with the founding of Israel and the United States, both of which involved serious crimes against the peoples who lived on the lands that were overrun and colonized. Not surprisingly, Israeli and American elites have gone to substantial lengths to whitewash this cruel history. But there is little hand wringing about this issue in the United States today, mainly because the controversial events happened so long ago that it seems like ancient history. Israel's creation, on the other hand, is much more recent, and how it happened is a remarkably contentious subject, not just because the Palestinians have a growing voice in the discourse, but also because a handful of scholars (many of whom are Israeli) have challenged Israel's founding myths. As one might expect, most Israelis and most of their American supporters have not changed their thinking about Israel's birth, but instead have redoubled their efforts to sell the myths.

CHAPTER 7

Liberal Lies

There is a well-developed body of norms that prescribe acceptable forms of state behavior and proscribe unacceptable conduct in both peacetime and wartime. These norms are closely linked to just-war theory and liberal ideology more generally, and many of them are codified in international law.

Most statesmen claim that they accept these liberal norms and invariably emphasize their commitment to the rule of law. Nevertheless, leaders sometimes conclude that their national interest compels them to act in ways that contradict these rules. This behavior includes invading other countries for strategic gain and launching preventive wars, as well as waging war in vicious ways that violate just-war theory. For example, Duke political scientist Alexander Downes shows in his seminal book *Targeting Civilians in War* that "desperation to win and to save lives on one's own side in costly, protracted wars of attrition causes belligerents to target enemy civilians."[1] Indeed, he shows that "democracies are some-what more likely than non-democracies to target civilians." Remember that the United States purposely killed about 900,000 Japanese civilians in the last five months of World War II, not because it feared losing the war, but because it wanted to win the war without having to invade the Japanese homeland.[2] General Curtis LeMay, who was in charge of that murderous bombing campaign, once remarked, "If we'd lost the war, we'd all have been prosecuted as war criminals."[3]

Such brutal state behavior, however, is not restricted to wartime. The United States, for example, played the leading role in getting the UN to impose economic sanctions on Iraq from August 1990 until May 2003. That financial and trade embargo helped create a humanitarian disaster, killing about 500,000 Iraqi civilians according to UNICEF estimates.[4] Statesmen also form alliances with particularly odious countries when they believe that it makes good strategic sense. To defeat Nazi Germany in World War II, both Prime Minister Winston Churchill and President Franklin D. Roosevelt worked closely with Josef Stalin, who was not simply a tyrant, but was also one of the greatest mass murderers of all time.[5]

When states act in ways that run counter to liberal norms or international law, their leaders often invent false stories that are designed to mask what they are doing. Not surprisingly, both British and American elites—including academics, journalists, and policymakers—went to considerable lengths during World War II to portray Stalin in a favorable light, so that it would not appear that Britain and the United States were run by ruthless statesmen who would cooperate with one tyrannical mass murderer to defeat another.[6] Thus, he was frequently described as friendly "Uncle Joe," while the stark differences between the American and Soviet political systems were sometimes played down, giving the impression that the Soviet Union was a democracy too.

The Western allies' efforts to portray Stalin as something he was not was put to a severe test in the spring of 1943, when it became apparent to both Churchill and Roosevelt that the Soviets had murdered thousands of Poles—most of whom were army officers—in the Katyn Forest three years earlier in the spring of 1940.[7] As one British policymaker remarked at the time, "It is obviously a very awkward matter when we are fighting for a moral cause and when we intend to deal adequately with war criminals, that our Allies should be open to accusations of this kind."[8] Nevertheless, the British government went right to work blaming the killings on Nazi Germany, knowing that the Soviets were actually responsible. The Foreign Office maintained that "the story should be treated as a German attempt to undermine allied solidarity," while the Political Warfare Executive, a key government unit involved in the propaganda war, issued a directive saying: "It is our job to help to ensure that history will record the Katyn Forest incident as a futile attempt by Germany to postpone defeat by political methods."[9]

Another case of liberal lies involves Nazi Germany's efforts to blame Poland for starting World War II on September 1, 1939. On that fateful day, Hitler told the Reichstag that he had been patiently waiting for two days "for the Polish government to send a plenipotentiary" to talk with him, but none arrived.[10] The clear implication was that he was interested in finding a diplomatic solution to the dispute between the two countries over the future of Danzig and the Polish Corridor, but Poland would not cooperate with him, because its leaders were not interested in peace. Then, after mentioning his "love of peace," Hitler claimed that Poland had fired the first shots at targets in Germany, and that the Wehrmacht was merely "returning the fire." Germany, in other words, was acting in self-defense. In fact, Germany had staged a series of border incidents on the evening of August 31 that were designed to make it look like Poland started the war, when it was actually the victim of Nazi aggression.

A final example concerns the British aerial-bombing strategy against Germany during World War II. Beginning in the early spring of 1942, Bomber Command began a sustained area-bombing campaign, which guaranteed that many German civilians would die. The British government did not want to tell its public that it was purposely killing civilians, because this was a gross violation of the laws of war. Instead, officials lied and said that the attacks were confined to military targets, because "the intentional bombardment of civilian populations, as such, is forbidden." As the historian Max Hastings notes, "From beginning to end of the war, ministers prevaricated—indeed, lied flatly again and again— about the nature of the bomber offensive."[11]

WHY ELITES TELL LIBERAL LIES

One might think that there is little need to tell liberal lies, since most people intuitively understand that international politics is a nasty and dangerous business, and that countries sometimes have good reason to act in ways that are contrary to liberal norms or international law. While there is an element of truth in that argument, the fact is that most people still prefer to think—whenever they can—that their country is acting justly while their adversaries are not. Thus, leaders sometimes lie to cover up their country's ruthless behavior because their publics simply do not want to hear the truth. The logic here is similar to the one that underpins nationalist mythmaking. Of course, leaders themselves are often moved to lie because they want to portray themselves as responsible and law-abiding members of the international community, and sometimes because they fear being brought to trial down the road. Even Osama bin Laden felt the need to explain why Al Qaeda was justified in killing thousands of civilians on September 11.[12]

The fact is that many people around the world identify with the well-established body of liberal norms and rules that are supposed to guide state behavior, and they want to believe that their government acts in accordance with them. Political theorist Michael Walzer captures this point when he writes: "The clearest evidence for the stability of our values over time is the unchanging character of the lies soldiers and statesmen tell. They lie in order to justify themselves, and so they describe for us the lineaments of justice."[13]

Furthermore, as with nationalist mythmaking, leaders tell liberal lies to gain legitimacy abroad. But the payoffs here are likely to be just as small for the same reasons. Outsiders are likely to have a good appreciation of what actually happened in the events that are being lied about and therefore be hard to fool. Of course, it might occasionally be possible to deceive a lot of people in a friendly country who have strong incentives—be they ideological or strategic—for believing certain liberal falsehoods. In short, liberal lies are hard to sell abroad, especially when they involve recent events.

WHEN LIBERAL LYING IS LIKELY

Virtually all leaders—whether they head up autocracies or democracies—are wont to justify their behavior in terms of liberal norms and international law, even when their actions are principally motivated by the kind of hard-headed strategic calculations identified with realism. However, this penchant for liberal rhetoric does not create problems as long as a country's behavior is consistent with both realist and liberal dictates, as it often is. For example, America's participation in the fights against Imperial Japan and Nazi Germany in World War II was easily defensible on moral as well as strategic grounds. The same could be said of the United States' decision to contain the Soviet Union during the Cold War, or to go to war against Iraq in 1991.

Problems arise, however, when realist and idealist imperatives are at odds with each other. In those cases, elites will usually act like realists and talk like liberals, which invariably necessitates deception, including lying.

CHAPTER 8

The Downside of Telling International Lies

Up to now, I have focused on the potential benefits of international lying. The emphasis has been on showing what leaders might gain for their country by telling lies to other countries or to their own people. However, there are costs as well as benefits associated with the different types of international lies that I have identified. There can even be a price to pay when a lie works as intended.

To assess the negative aspects of international lying—and please remember that I am looking at the matter from a strictly utilitarian perspective—it is necessary to consider how each of the five kinds of lies affects a country's domestic politics as well as its foreign policy. Different criteria are needed to evaluate the possible negative effects of lying in each realm. Let me start by describing the main criterion for domestic politics.

Pervasive lying will inevitably do grave damage to any body politic, because it creates a poisonous culture of dishonesty.[1] Therefore, it makes eminently good sense for leaders and their fellow citizens to work to minimize the amount of lying that takes place in their country. This is not a simple task, however, because there are sometimes powerful incentives for individuals to lie and cheat to get ahead, even though such selfish behavior is bad for the society at large. Just think about Bernie Madoff, the Wall Street investor who defrauded thousands of clients of billions of dollars. Of course, he is not lacking for company, which is why governments monitor and regulate the behavior of their citizenry in various realms, and why the elites in most societies routinely condemn lying about domestic political and economic matters.

Given this situation, telling international lies raises a potential danger that is deeply worrisome. Specifically, there is the possibility that lying about matters relating to foreign policy might have a blowback effect on everyday life inside a country's borders. In other words, lying about international politics in a visible way—even if it makes good strategic sense—might spill into the national arena and cause significant trouble by legitimizing and encouraging dishonesty in daily life. Too much concealment and spinning can also have unfortunate consequences, but those kinds of deception are not nearly as dangerous as rampant lying.

Routine lying has at least four dangerous consequences for life on the home front, all of which are especially serious for democracies. Widespread lying makes it difficult for citizens in a democracy to make informed choices when they vote on issues and candidates, simply because there is a good chance that they are basing their decisions on false information. How can a voter hold a politician or leader accountable when it is impossible to know the truth about that person's actions? Democracies operate best when they include a reasonably efficient marketplace of ideas, which can only work when citizens have reliable information and there are high levels of transparency and honesty.

Lying by government officials—to each other or the public—can also cripple a state's policy-making process, whether it is a democracy or not.[2] The main reason is that the transaction costs in a world of deceit are enormous, because policymakers cannot trust each other, and thus they have to devote extra time and resources to making sure that the information they have at their disposal is accurate. But even when they perform due diligence, they still might not get all of their facts correct, in which case their decisions will be based on false information, which would greatly increase the chances of pursuing wrongheaded policies.

Furthermore, promiscuous lying can undermine the rule of law, which is at the heart of democratic life. Patrick J. Fitzgerald, the special prosecutor who indicted White House aide Lewis "Scooter" Libby in October 2006 for lying about his role in revealing the identity of a CIA aide, put the point well when he said: "The truth is the engine of our judicial system. And if you compromise the truth, the whole process is lost."[3] Of course, laws exist in part to punish lying, which means that some modicum of dishonesty is expected in any society. But lying cannot be widespread; there has to be a substantial amount of honesty and trust in public life for any legal system to work effectively. Consider, for example, that George Ryan, the former governor of Illinois, who initially favored capital punishment, felt that he had to suspend all executions in his state because there was convincing evidence that many of the inmates on death row were convicted on the basis of lies and other improprieties.[4]

Finally, if lying is pervasive in a democracy, it might alienate the public to the point where it loses faith in democratic government and is willing to countenance some form of authoritarian rule. After all, it is hard to see how a democracy can remain viable for long if the people have no respect for their leaders, because they think they are a bunch of liars, and no respect for their institutions, because they think that they are deeply corrupt. In short, too much lying can do serious damage to any body politic.

Switching gears, how might international lying adversely affect a country's foreign policy? As emphasized, leaders lie to each other and to their own people because they believe that doing so serves the national interest. And the sad fact is that lying sometimes does make good strategic sense. If it did not, there would be no good justification for the various kinds of lies described in the previous chapters. Nevertheless, lying occasionally backfires, in which case a country might end up worse off rather than better off for having told a particular lie. Hence, the key question for assessing the ramifications of international lying is: which types of lies are most likely to backfire and have harmful strategic consequences?

In sum, the *potential for blowback* is the main criterion for assessing the consequences of international lying on the home front, while the *potential for backfiring* and doing a state more harm than good is the paramount criterion in the foreign-policy realm.

THE DANGERS OF INTER-STATE LYING

Inter-state lying is unlikely to cause serious trouble at home. The danger of blowback is minimal in part because leaders do not lie to each other very often. The main reason, however, is that most people understand that the rulebook for international politics is different from the one used in domestic politics. In particular, they understand that leaders sometimes have to lie and cheat in their dealings with other countries, especially when they are dealing with a dangerous adversary. For better or for worse, lying is widely accepted as a necessary, albeit distasteful, tool of foreign policy. This is why statesmen and diplomats are rarely punished when they get caught telling inter-state lies. In contrast, lying is generally considered to be wrong when the issue at hand is national in scope, mainly because a country's survival is seldom at stake when domestic politics are at play.

It might seem unrealistic to think that inter-state lying can be compartmentalized the way I describe it without encouraging or legitimizing lying on the home front. But that would be wrong; reasonably clear boundaries can be drawn that stipulate when lying is acceptable and when it is not. Remember that most of us accept the fact that there are exceptional circumstances where we are allowed to lie in our daily lives without that becoming accepted behavior in ordinary circumstances. For example, when I was a cadet at West Point in the late 1960s, there was a strict honor code, which emphatically stated that a cadet does not lie, cheat, or steal, nor tolerate those who do. Nevertheless, we were allowed to tell white lies—it was called "social honor"—in instances where we might hurt someone else's feelings over a trivial matter. To cite a popular example from the time: if you went to your tactical officer's home and his wife served a dreadful meal, it was acceptable to tell her that the meal was delicious. We clearly understood, however, that telling lies in awkward social situations like that one did not give us license to lie in other circumstances.

As noted, the same logic applies to people bargaining over a house or car. They are allowed to lie about their reservation price—it is part of the game—but that does not mean that they are free to lie in their other matters. Inter-state politics is another well-defined domain where lying is generally considered acceptable, and where there is not much danger of spillover or blowback.

Turning to the international consequences, there is no doubt that inter-state lying can backfire, just as any policy a state pursues can fail and harm the national interest. But there is nothing special about this particular kind of international lie that makes it prone to backfiring, as I will argue is the case with fearmongering and strategic cover-ups. Moreover, the damage done when inter-state lying goes awry is usually not major, which is not to deny that there are some costs.

A lie that a statesman or diplomat tells to another country can go wrong in two different ways. First, it might be exposed soon after it is told, which would obviously make it impossible for the lie to have its intended effect. But what about the consequences for the leaders who lied? They are unlikely to be severe because the incentive to retaliate would not be great, since the lie was uncovered before it could do harm to the target country, and since there are usually not good ways for the intended victim to punish the liars. One possible option is to embarrass the liar, but that is a minor punishment indeed. And that sanction is not even likely to work well, since most people understand that leaders sometimes lie to each other for the good of their countries. It is hard to shame a leader with that motive, even if he botches the job and gets caught red-handed.

The target state might retaliate by ending ongoing negotiations or pursuing hard-line policies against the country that tried to dupe it. In that case, the exposed lie would seriously worsen relations between the involved countries. However, this is unlikely to happen, not only because the lie was exposed and failed to harm the intended target, but also because—as I have emphasized repeatedly—it is taken for granted that states lie to each other. There is no question that an unmasked lie could contribute to the deterioration of relations between two states, but it is highly unlikely that it would be the main driving force, which would almost certainly be some significant economic or political dispute between them.

A case of backfiring that fits this profile occurred when the Eisenhower administration was caught telling a handful of blatant lies about the U-2 incident in the spring of 1960.[5] The president himself felt humiliated when those lies were revealed, but more importantly, he was preparing at the time to meet with his Soviet counterpart, Nikita Khrushchev. Both leaders were hoping to improve relations between the superpowers and slow down the nuclear arms race. But the planned summit was scuttled, in part because of the administration's lies about the plane's mission. The main reason it failed, however, was that the incident revealed to the world that the United States was violating Soviet airspace and operating spy planes over the Soviet Union, which caused Khrushchev significant political problems at home and made it difficult for him to meet and cooperate with Eisenhower. In short, the lies that the president and his advisors told to Moscow mattered, but not that much.

One might argue that getting caught telling a lie hurts a state's reputation, which can cause serious damage to its international position. As noted, reputation is important in the realm of low politics.[6] If a country made a practice of telling lies when dealing with economic and mundane political issues, it would quickly develop a reputation for dishonesty, which would discourage other countries from interacting and cooperating with it. But this is one reason why there is little inter-state lying when low politics are involved, which, of course, renders the reputation issue of little practical significance in this domain.

In the realm of high politics, where lying seems to be more frequent but still not commonplace, reputation does not matter much.[7] Whenever an issue directly involves a country's security, its leaders cannot afford to pay much attention to the reputation of other states, largely because they can never be sure that they will not be duped by a state with a good reputation. Just because a state has been honest ten times does not mean it will be honest the eleventh time. Being played for a sucker does not matter much when low politics are in play, but it could have disastrous consequences if a country's survival is at stake. Thus, when leaders are dealing with issues that involve national security, they largely discount the past behavior of other states, which effectively means that a damaged reputation is usually not a serious price to pay for getting caught in a lie.

An inter-state lie can backfire in a second way. Specifically, the deceit can go undetected for a long enough time for the intended target to be bamboozled by the false story; nevertheless, the lie does not work as intended and leaves the country that told it worse off than it would have been had it not lied. In other words, a leader can successfully tell a misconceived lie. A good example of this phenomenon is Khrushchev's lies about the Soviet missile force in the late 1950s. He greatly exaggerated Soviet capabilities to convince the United States not to threaten or attack the Soviet Union, and more generally to respect Moscow's interests and wishes around the world. But instead, the alleged missile gap scared the United States and caused it to significantly escalate the arms race at a time when Khrushchev was hoping to slow it down so that Moscow could spend more money on economic and social programs. As this case shows, even well-told lies sometimes backfire because the policy that they underpin is badly flawed.

THE PERILS OF FEARMONGERING

Fearmongering—unlike the lies that leaders tell each other—is likely to have serious negative consequences for both a state's internal politics and its foreign policy. To start, there is considerable potential for blowback. Leaders who engage in fearmongering betray a certain contempt for their people and for democracy more generally. After all, they are lying because they do not think that their fellow citizens can be trusted to understand and support the right foreign policy, even if they are given a straightforward assessment of the threat environment. Trying to present the facts of the situation even more clearly and more forcefully will not work either. Therefore, to ensure that the country adopts the correct foreign policy, it is necessary to inflate the threat by deploying lies about the adversary and engaging in other forms of deception.

The problem with this kind of behavior is that the leadership's low regard for the public is likely to spill over into the domestic realm. Once a country's leaders conclude that its citizens do not understand important foreign policy issues and thus need to be manipulated, it is not much of a leap to apply the same sort of thinking to national issues. In essence, fearmongering makes it difficult to build a firewall between domestic and foreign policy, because the relationship between leaders and their people is basically the same in both domains. This is not to deny that the imperative to deceive is likely to be greater when foreign policy issues are on the table, because of the obvious link with the country's security.

Fearmongering is also prone to backfiring and producing foreign-policy fiascos. The root of the problem is that the public debate about the threat environment cannot help but be distorted, since the leaders are purposely deceiving their people about the dangers facing their country. In essence, they do not think that an honest threat assessment is enough to get the public to do the right thing. Of course, there may be circumstances where the public is an obstacle to dealing effectively with a serious threat, and thus it makes good strategic sense for leaders to engage in fearmongering. Indeed, a good case can be made that Roosevelt's lying about the *Greer* incident in 1941 was in the national interest, because the American people did not fully appreciate the danger that Nazi Germany presented to the United States.[8]

But it is also possible—maybe even likely—that the public is basically intelligent and responsible, and the reason that government leaders are having difficulty making their case is that they are misreading the threat and pushing a misguided policy. This outcome is especially likely if the government is facing substantial opposition from outside experts as well as the broader population. It seems likely that leaders offering sound arguments would be able to defend them in the marketplace of ideas—most of the time anyway—and not have to lie to the public, especially those experts who know the issue at hand. The fact that a leader feels compelled to fearmonger means that there is a good chance he is misreading the threat environment and that the public has gauged it correctly. If that is the case, and the government ends up pursuing a misguided policy, it will almost certainly lead to serious trouble.

Furthermore, if leaders lie in the service of promoting a flawed policy, they are likely to lose popular support when the public discovers that it has been misled, compounding the country's troubles. This is what happened to the Johnson administration during the Vietnam War and the Bush administration during the Iraq war. In each case, it became apparent when the war was going badly that there had been serious deception in the run-up to the conflict. Nevertheless, if statesmen and diplomats are found out to have lied about a policy that clearly achieves its aims, the public is unlikely to punish them, simply because nothing succeeds like success in international politics. Of course, that logic helps convince policymakers in the first place that they can get away with fearmongering.

THE HAZARDS OF STRATEGIC COVER-UPS

Strategic cover-ups can also lead to serious trouble both at home and abroad. Leaders who lie to their own citizens about either failed or contentious policies obviously think that their people are unable to deal intelligently with those matters. As with fearmongering, that situation is naturally ripe for blowback, because policymakers who hold such views can easily slide into thinking that the public is incapable of dealing intelligently with important domestic issues as well, which would open the floodgates for lying on the home front. That outcome would surely have regrettable consequences for any body politic.

How trouble might occur in the foreign policy realm depends on the type of cover-up and how it plays out. Let us first consider how concealing a controversial policy might backfire. A leader might decide to surreptitiously adopt a particular policy after an open and contentious public debate leads him to conclude that the policy in question is good for the country, even though it is deeply unpopular with a substantial portion of the citizenry. Alternatively, a leader might feel compelled to secretly adopt a policy before it is vigorously debated in public, simply because he anticipates that it would encounter serious opposition. In both scenarios, the leader would have to lie if he were asked whether the shrouded policy had been adopted.

There is serious potential for backfire with cover-ups of this sort, because whenever leaders cannot sell a policy to their public in a rational-legal manner, there is a good chance that the problem is with the policy, not the audience. This is especially true if a substantial number of outside experts oppose or are likely to oppose the policy in question. With the first scenario, however, there is at least a public debate where the leaders are forced to listen and respond to their critics' concerns, including those of outside experts who know the issues well. That back-and-forth is likely to make those leaders think hard about their preferred course of action, which reduces the likelihood that they are just covering up a misguided policy. Moreover, they might come to recognize certain problems with their preferred policy and modify it in smart ways. But in the second scenario, where there is hardly any public debate, the likelihood that a leader will recognize the flaws in his chosen policy is sharply reduced, and thus there is a greater possibility that it will go wrong.

Turning next to the other kind of strategic cover-up—hiding a failed policy—it might seem at first glance that backfiring is a moot issue, since the policy has already gone awry. But that conclusion would be wrong. Covering up a botched policy, which invariably entails protecting the responsible individuals and not firing them on the spot, is likely to mean that the failed policy—or some variant of it—will remain in place for a while, which is not a desirable outcome. For example, defending Marshal Joffre and his strategy for fighting the German army at Verdun meant that he and his flawed formula remained in place for the entire ten months of that bloody battle. France's soldiers would have been better served if a more able commander had replaced Joffre early in that fight.

Furthermore, hiding botched policies can lead to further disasters down the road, not just because incompetents are usually kept in key leadership positions for at least some period of time, but also because engaging in cover-ups makes it difficult to have a national security system in which policymakers and military commanders are held accountable for their actions. No organization can work effectively without accountability at every level of the operation. Finally, if a botched policy is kept under tight wraps, it is difficult to have a meaningful discussion about what went wrong and how best to make sure that it does not happen again.

In sum, strategic cover-ups may sometimes be necessary, but they carry significant risks, because they have considerable potential for backfiring as well as corrupting daily life on the home front.

THE RISKS OF NATIONALIST MYTHMAKING

Lying to help perpetrate national myths is unlikely to have harmful domestic or foreign-policy consequences. There is not much danger of blowback because most people are usually so taken with their nation's myths that they do not recognize them for what they are. Instead, they see the myths as hallowed truths, not lies or distortions of the historical record. George Orwell captures the essence of this collective self-delusion when he writes, "Nationalism is power-hunger tempered by self-deception. Every nationalist is capable of the most flagrant dishonesty, but he is also—since he is conscious of serving something bigger than himself—unshakably certain of being in the right."[9] Even well-educated and otherwise sophisticated elites sometimes fall victim to this phenomenon; in effect, they end up believing their own lies, in which case they are no longer lies. As the scholar Richard Neustadt notes, "The tendency of bureaucratic language to create in private the same images presented to the public never should be underrated."[10]

What about foreign policy? A number of prominent scholars, including Yale historian Paul Kennedy and Stephen Van Evera, maintain that nationalist myths sometimes lead states to behave foolishly.[11] Indeed, these kinds of myths are said to cause countries to act aggressively toward their neighbors and to refuse to resolve conflicts that are otherwise amenable to a peaceful settlement. Nationalist myths, for example, are said to be a major cause of Germany's aggressive behavior in the early part of the twentieth century—including starting World War I. Chauvinistic myths about Israel's history are said to be one of the main reasons that Israelis will not permit the Palestinians to have a viable state of their own, which makes it impossible to put an end to their longstanding conflict.

This perspective is wrong, however, because the causal arrow goes in the opposite direction: foreign policy behavior drives the creation of nationalist myths, not the other way around. Specifically, the rhetoric of nationalism is tailored to suit the behavior of states, which is driven largely by other calculations. For example, Germany's aggressive behavior in the years leading up to World War I was driven mainly by concerns about the European balance of power, and the national myths that it deployed back then were largely designed to justify its belligerent actions.[12] Israel's efforts to control all of what was once called Mandatory Palestine and deny the Palestinians a state of their own has been a central part of the Zionist agenda since its inception in the late 1880s.[13] Israel's actions since its founding in 1948 have been largely consistent with that original Zionist vision, and have not been driven in any meaningful way by the various nationalist myths that Israelis have invented. The main purpose of those false stories has been to whitewash Israel's brutal behavior toward the Palestinians, so that Israelis and their allies abroad think that Israel is always right and the Palestinians always wrong.

None of this is to deny that nationalism can be a potent cause of war. Indeed, it has been the most powerful ideology in the world over the past two centuries, and it has played a key role in tearing some states and empires apart, and has also led some countries to start wars with their neighbors. For example, Bismarck was motivated by nationalism as well as security concerns when he started and won wars in 1864, 1866, and 1870.[14] His goal was not simply to expand Prussia's borders and make it more secure, but also to create a unified German state. And remember that Zionism is effectively

Jewish nationalism, and there was no way that the Zionists coming from Europe could create a Jewish state in all of Palestine without behaving aggressively toward the people who were already living in the region. So nationalism is clearly a major cause of war, but the myths that accompany it are not. At most, they have a secondary or tertiary effect on the making of a country's foreign policy.

THE POTENTIAL COSTS OF LIBERAL LIES

Liberal lies also do not have a significant downside either at home or on the foreign-policy front. The same shared self-delusion that attends nationalist mythmaking tends to work here as well: most people do not recognize that lying is taking place, because they are inclined to believe that their own country almost always acts nobly. Thus, there is not much danger of blowback. But even in those rare instances when liberal lies do not work as intended and the public recognizes that their country has acted in an immoral or illegal way, there is not much danger of blowback, because most people understand that the rule book used in international politics is not the same one used inside their country's borders.

The liberal lies that leaders tell also have little effect on how their country acts in the international arena. The same logic that underpins nationalist mythmaking applies here: statesmen and diplomats invariably do whatever they think is necessary to maximize their country's security, regardless of what language they have employed to explain past and present actions. In other words, the causal arrow runs from foreign policy behavior to liberal rhetoric, not the other way around.

CHAPTER 9

Conclusion

It is clear from the historical record that although lying is often condemned as shameful behavior, leaders of all kinds think that it is a useful tool of statecraft that can and should be employed in a variety of circumstances.

Leaders not only tell lies to other countries, they also lie to their own people, and they do so because they believe it is in the best interest of their country. And sometimes they are right. Who would argue that statesman and diplomats should not lie to a dangerous adversary—especially in wartime—if their deceptions deliver strategic benefits? Probably the best example of where lying played an important role in helping a country shift the balance of power in its favor was when Bismarck's falsehoods helped cause France to start a war with Prussia in 1870. Prussia won a decisive victory, which led to the creation of a powerful Germany in the heart of Europe.

Moreover, it occasionally makes good sense for leaders to lie to their own people. It seems to me, for example, that President Kennedy was right to lie to the American people about the deal he cut with the Soviets on the Jupiter missiles in Turkey, since that lie helped settle the Cuban Missile Crisis and avert a possible war between the nuclear-armed superpowers.

Lying does not always work, however. It is difficult for leaders to snooker other states, because inter-state lies are usually directed at potential or real adversaries who are understandably suspicious of anything their opponents might say about matters relating to their security. This lack of trust between rival states explains in good part why there is not much lying between them. It was hard for someone like Churchill or Roosevelt to get away with lying to Hitler, or visa versa—and certainly not for long—because they were just too suspicious of each other. Although it is easier for a leader to lie to his public—because people tend to trust their own government—lying to fellow citizens does not always work either. For example, Roosevelt lied about the *Greer* incident in 1941 to help get the United States more deeply involved in World War II. But his lies had hardly any effect on the American public, which remained in an isolationist mood until Pearl Harbor.

Failure to hoodwink the intended target is not the only thing that can go wrong when leaders tell international lies. There is also the danger that their lies will be exposed and harm rather than help their country, as happened when the Eisenhower administration told a series of lies after the Soviet Union had shot down a U-2 spy plane. Of course, lies can backfire even if they are not exposed and are believed by the leaders of the target country. This is what happened when Khrushchev exaggerated the size of the Soviet ICBM arsenal in the late 1950s. He ended up fueling an arms race which he did not want and which was not in his country's best interest. The Johnson administration's lying about events in the Gulf of Tonkin in August 1964 is another case where a well-told set of lies backfired. Those falsehoods played an important role in getting the United States into the Vietnam War. Similarly, the Bush administration told various lies in the run-up to the March 2003 invasion of Iraq, which were not exposed at the time and helped sell the case for toppling Saddam Hussein from power. In both of those cases, the fearmongering led to strategic disasters for the United States.

Backfiring is just one potential downside of international lying; the other is blowback, and it is the more worrisome of the two. Leaders who lie to their citizenry for what they believe are good strategic reasons might nevertheless do significant damage to their body politic by fostering a culture of dishonesty. This is why fearmongering and strategic cover-ups are the most dangerous kinds of lies that leaders can tell. Both carry a risk of blowback because they involve leaders lying to their publics, and both are also prone to producing foreign-policy debacles. The potential costs associated with the other three kinds of international lies—nationalist mythmaking, liberal lies, and inter-state lies—are not nearly as great as with fearmongering and strategic cover-ups.

What lessons can we draw for future American foreign policy from this examination of international lying? The United States emerged from the Cold War as the most powerful state in the world. That situation is not likely to change in the foreseeable future, as there is only one state—China—that could challenge America's position of primacy. But China has a long way to go before it catches up, and it has problems that may slow or even halt its climb to the top.[1] At the same time, a large portion of the American foreign-policy establishment—including Democrats and Republicans—believes that the United States has a moral as well as strategic responsibility not only to police the entire globe, but to try to shape the politics of individual countries. Moreover, American leaders have not been shy about using military force to achieve their grand goals. The United States has fought five wars since the Cold War ended in 1989, and it has been at war for fourteen of the subsequent twenty-two years: 1991 against Iraq; 1995 and 1999 against Sebia; 2001–2002 against Afghanistan; 2003–2011 against both Afghanistan and Iraq.

The ongoing wars in Afghanistan and Iraq will surely dampen the foreign-policy elite's enthusiasm for reshaping the world at the end of a rifle barrel, but it remains to be seen how much. As a result, it may not be long before the United States marches off on another crusade. There is little reason to think that its basic commitment to running the world will go away anytime soon, which means that United States is going to be deeply involved in global politics for the foreseeable future.

Such an ambitious foreign policy is likely to create numerous situations in the years ahead where America's leaders feel compelled to fearmonger. Remember, the leaders who are most likely to lie to their publics are those who head democracies bent on fighting wars of choice in distant places. That description obviously fits the United States, and it goes a long way toward explaining the Bush administration's deceptions in the run-up to the 2003 Iraq war. But it was certainly not the first administration to engage in fearmongering and it will not be the last. The United States spends more on its military than the rest of the world put together; it has a robust nuclear deterrent and is insulated from most dangers by two enormous oceans. Given how secure America really is, the only way its leaders can justify ambitious global crusades is to convince the American people that relatively minor problems are in fact dire and growing dangers. Given America's global ambitions, therefore, we should expect fearmongering to be a constant feature of its national security discourse in the years ahead. This is bad news, because fearmongering not only can have a corrosive effect on democratic institutions, it can also lead to disasters like Iraq and Vietnam.

Notes

Preface

1. Mary Dalrymple, "Kerry Avoids Calling Bush 'Liar,'" *MSNBC.com,*
   September 24, 2004, http://www.msnbc.msn.com/id/6086823;
   David Stout, "Kerry Accuses Bush of Hiding the Truth about Iraq,"
   New York Times, September 16, 2004. "Transcript: First Presidential
   Debate," *Washington Post,* September 30, 2004. However, as
   Dalrymple points out, others involved in the Kerry campaign did
   not hesitate to call Bush a liar, and Kerry himself did on occasion
   call Bush a liar, although he was clearly reluctant to use that word.
   Patrick Healy, "Kerry Camp Lowers N.H. Expectations: Behind
   in Polls, Senator Now Seeks Spot in 'Top Two,'" *Boston Globe,*
   December 8 2003.

Introduction

1. Charles A. Duelfer, *Comprehensive Report of the Special Advisor to the
   DCI on Iraq's WMD,* Vol. 1 (Washington, DC: Central Intelligence
   Agency, September 30, 2004), 34–35. See also Julian Borger,
   "Interrogators 'Botched Hunt for Iraq's WMD,'" *Guardian,* April 27,
   2005; Rupert Cornwell, "Saddam Was Bluffing over WMD Stocks,
   Says Report," *Independent,* October 2, 2003; Johanna McGeary,
   Timothy J. Burger, and Elaine Shannon, "What Saddam Was Really
   Thinking," *Time,* October 18, 2004, http://www.time.com/time/
   magazine/article/0,9171,995422,00.html; Walter Pincus and Dana
   Priest, "Hussein's Weapons May Have Been Bluff," *Washington Post,*
   October 1, 2003; Alec Russell, "Leaked Report Points to Saddam
   WMD Bluff," *Telegraph,* October 2, 2003.

2. George Tenet, *At the Center of the Storm: My Years at the CIA* (New York: Harper Collins, 2007), 331–33.

3. Duelfer, *Comprehensive Report,* 34.

4. In an article discussing "Saddam's alleged weapons bluff," Slobodan Lekic writes, "Publicly Saddam denied having unconventional weapons. But from 1998 until 2002, he prevented UN inspectors from working in the country and when they finally returned in November 2002, they often complained that Iraq wasn't fully cooperating." Slobodan Lekic, "Aide: Saddam Did Get Rid of Iraq WMD," Associated Press, August 2, 2003. There is no question that Saddam denied the weapons inspectors access to Iraq between 1998 and 2002, but that is not evidence of bluffing. While the inspectors did sometimes complain about not gaining quick access to certain locations after returning to Iraq, the problems were eventually resolved and the UN was confident that it could assess whether Iraq had WMD if given sufficient time to scour the country. The Bush administration, however, forced the inspectors to leave Iraq before they finished the job so that the United States could invade that country and remove Saddam from power.

5. Not everyone accepts the argument that it is right to lie to protect an innocent person, as is evident from well-known case of the "lying Baptists." In 1804, a debate broke out in a Baptist congregation in Kentucky over whether it was permissible for a man to lie about whether he had a wife and children to marauding Indians who would probably kill them. In other words, was it right to lie to protect your family in the face of grave danger? The congregation actually split over the matter, with "truthful Baptists" on one side and "lying Baptists" on the other.

6. Lanse P. Minkler and Thomas J. Miceli, "Lying, Integrity, and Cooperation," *Review of Social Economy* 62, no. 1 (March 2004): 27–50.

7. For a powerful statement against lying of almost every sort, see Sissela Bok, *Lying: Moral Choice in Public and Private Life,* 2nd ed. (New York: Vintage Books, 1999).

8. Kenneth N. Waltz, *Theory of International Politics* (Reading, MA: Addison-Wesley, 1979), chap. 5.

9. Thomas Hobbes, *Leviathan,* ed. C. B. Macpherson (Harmondsworth, UK: Penguin, 1985), 202.

10. On the pervasiveness of deception, see: Larry Alexander and Emily Sherwin, "Deception in Morality and Law," *Law and Philosophy* 22, no. 5 (September 2003): 393–450; F. G. Bailey, *The Prevalence of Deceit* (Ithaca, NY: Cornell University Press, 1991); J. A. Barnes, *A Pack of Lies: Towards a Sociology of Lying* (Cambridge, UK: Cambridge University Press, 1994); Paul Ekman, *Telling Lies: Clues to Deceit in the Marketplace, Politics, and Marriage* (New York: Norton, 1985); Michael Lewis and Carolyn Saarni, eds., *Lying and Deception in Everyday Life* (New York: Guilford, 1993); Clancy Martin, ed., *The Philosophy of Deception* (New York: Oxford University Press, 2009); David Nyberg, *The Varnished Truth: Truth Telling and Deceiving in Ordinary Life* (Chicago: University of Chicago Press, 1993); Loyal Rue, *By the Grace of Guile: The Role of Deception in Natural History and Human Affairs* (New York: Oxford University Press, 1994).

11. That individual would be lying, however, if he purposely left out information that was requested on the job application form. He is obligated in such cases to reveal all the relevant information. For example, in the spring of 1995, Harvard University rescinded its offer of admission to a young woman who did not report that she had been found guilty of killing her mother in 1990. Harvard officials felt that she had a responsibility to inform them of this matter in her application. Fox Butterfield, "Woman Who Killed Mother Denied Harvard Admission," *New York Times,* April 8, 1995.

12. Alexander and Sherwin write, "Moral philosophers frequently distinguish between lying and deception and condemn lying as the worse offense" ("Deception in Morality and Law," 400).

13. Eric Alterman, *When Presidents Lie: A History of Official Deception and Its Consequences* (New York: Viking, 2004). See also James P. Pfiffner, *The Character Factor: How We Judge America's Presidents* (College Station: Texas A & M University Press, 2004), chaps. 2–3; David Wise, *The Politics of Lying: Government Deception, Secrecy, and Power* (New York: Random House, 1973).

14. Immanuel Kant, *Ethical Philosophy,* trans. James W. Ellington (Indianapolis: Hackett, 1983), 90.

15. Although bluffing in this book is equated with lying, international-relations scholars also talk about countries bluffing by moving or deploying military forces in ways that falsely signals that they might be used. Even if these shows of force involve no lying, the goal is still to mislead another country. I do not consider such cases,

however, simply because no lying is involved. But if I did, I would be able to point to more cases of bluffing.

Chapter 1

1. This line of reasoning is evident in Section 1001 of Title 18 of the United States Code, which is the statute that criminalizes false statements. Specifically, "A statement can be considered false for 1001 purposes even though it is 'literally' true if it misleads federal agents." See Jae Youn John Kim, "False Statements," *American Criminal Law Review* 40, no. 2 (Spring 2003): 515.

2. Harry G. Frankfurt has written a highly regarded book, *On Bullshit* (Princeton, NJ: Princeton University Press, 2005), which might seem relevant for this book, but is not for two reasons. First, as the author makes clear, bullshitting is fundamentally different than lying. A bullshitter pays virtually no attention to whether or not he is telling the truth. "The truth-values of his statements are of no central interest to him....His intention is neither to report the truth nor to conceal it." (55) In the course of telling his story—usually a "panoramic" story—he may say some things that are false, but this is not lying because he is not purposely saying something that he knows to be untrue. (52) "His eye is not on the facts at all." (56) Liars, in contrast, pay careful attention to the facts, although they do not tell the truth about them. The liar "is attempting to lead us away from a correct apprehension of reality." (54–55) Second, there is little evidence of bullshitting in international politics, probably because it is usually easy to recognize and thus unlikely to have much of a payoff. As Frankfurt notes, "Most people are rather confident of their ability to recognize bullshit and to avoid being taken in by it. So the phenomenon has not aroused much deliberate concern, nor attracted much sustained inquiry." (1) He also notes that bullshitting is commonplace in good part because people often feel compelled "to speak extensively about matters of which they are to some degree ignorant." (63) Statesmen and diplomats rarely find themselves in that situation, which is not to deny that they sometimes make foolish decisions. In short, it does not make sense to treat bullshitting as a fourth category of deception.

3. Quoted in Corey Dade, Suzanne Vranica, and Kevin Helliker, "Woods Aims to Stem Damage," *Wall Street Journal,* December 3, 2009.

4. American Bar Association, *Model Rules of Professional Conduct,* August 2002, Rule 3.3 (a). See also Monroe H. Freedman, *Lawyers' Ethics in an Adversary System* (Indianapolis: Bobbs-Merrill, 1975); Robert J. Spitzer, *Saving the Constitution from Lawyers: How Legal Training and Law Reviews Distort Constitutional Meaning* (New York: Cambridge University Press, 2008), 11–14. It is worth noting that many legal scholars believe that "the adversary system assumes that the most efficient and fair way of determining the truth is by presenting the strongest possible case for each side of the controversy before an impartial judge or jury" (Freedman, *Ethics in an Adversary System,* 9). In other words, spinning by the rival lawyers is ultimately the best way to find the truth. But not all students of the law share that view. See Stephan Landsman, *Readings on Adversarial Justice: The American Approach to Adjudication* (St. Paul, MN: West, 1988), chap. 2.

5. James Risen, "Captives Deny Qaeda Worked with Baghdad," *New York Times,* June 9, 2003. There was further evidence from the intelligence community that cast doubt on the purported link between bin Laden and Saddam. See *Iraq on the Record: The Bush Administration's Public Statements on Iraq,* Report prepared for Congressman Henry A. Waxman by the Minority Staff, Committee on Government Reform, U.S. House of Representatives, March 16, 2004, 21–25.

6. According to the United States Code, concealment is criminal behavior when it involves a "trick, scheme, or device." In other words, there must be an "affirmative act of concealment." See Kim, "False Statements," 515. In my classification, such behavior would be akin to lying—indeed it would probably involve lying; it would not fit my definition of concealment, which does not involve an affirmative act.

7. Quoted in Albert Z. Carr, "Is Business Bluffing Ethical?" *Harvard Business Review,* January-February 1968, 143. For the case that bluffing in business transactions is not lying, see Thomas Carson, "Second Thoughts about Bluffing," *Business Ethics Quarterly* 3, no. 4 (October 1993): 317–41. For the other side in this debate, see Gary E. Jones, "Lying and Intentions," *Journal of Business Ethics* 5, no. 4 (August 1986): 347–49. See also Thomas L. Carson, "On the Definition of Lying: A Reply to Jones and Revisions," *Journal of Business Ethics* 7, no. 7 (July 1998): 509–14.

Chapter 2

1. Although the focus in this book is on the creation and promotion of nationalist myths by individual states, there is no question that ethnic groups that do not have their own state—either because they have never had one or because they lost it—also tell lies about their past. Thus, some of my arguments about nationalist mythmaking apply to stateless nations as well as nation-states themselves.

2. This kind of selfish behavior was on display during the Iran-Contra scandal, when senior members of the Reagan administration were investigated and some were charged with breaking the law. See Eric Alterman, *When Presidents Lie: A History of Official Deception and Its Consequences* (New York: Viking, 2004), chap. 5.

3. Threat deflation is another possible kind of strategic lie. In this case, a leader lies to his public to make a threat look less serious than it actually is. This behavior might come into play when a leader is determined to avoid war in the face of intense public pressure to the contrary. Threat deflation is not considered in this book, mainly because it rarely occurs.

Chapter 3

1. Quoted in J. A. Barnes, *A Pack of Lies: Towards a Sociology of Lying* (Cambridge, UK: Cambridge University Press, 1994), 23.

2. Sissela Bok, *Lying: Moral Choice in Public and Private Life,* 2nd ed. (New York: Vintage Books, 1999), xxiii.

3. Quoted in Avishai Margalit, "The Violent Life of Yitzhak Shamir," *New York Review of Books,* May 14, 1992, 23. Another Israeli prime minister, Moshe Sharett, once remarked: "I have learned that the state of Israel cannot be ruled in our generation without deceit and adventurism. These are historical facts that cannot be altered....In the end, history will justify both the stratagems of deceit and the acts of adventurism. All I know is that I, Moshe Sharett, am not capable of them, and I am therefore unsuited to lead the country." Quoted in Simha Flapan, *The Birth of Israel: Myths and Realities* (New York: Pantheon Books, 1987), 51–52.

4. Of course, this does not mean that leaders should axiomatically assume that foreign diplomats and statesman are lying to them, because that kind of paranoia would lead them to misread the

many situations in which they are being told the truth. Stalin
exhibited this kind of thinking in the spring of 1941, when he
foolishly dismissed warnings from Churchill and others about an
impending German attack on the Soviet Union. See Richard K.
Betts, *Surprise Attack: Lessons for Defense Planning* (Washington, DC:
Brookings Institution, 1982), 34–42; Gabriel Gorodetsky, *Grand
Delusion: Stalin and the German Invasion of Russia* (New Haven,
CT:Yale University Press, 1999), chap. 8; Barton Whaley, *Codeword
BARBAROSSA* (Cambridge, MA: MIT Press, 1974).

5. Charles Lipson, "International Cooperation in Economic and
Security Affairs," *World Politics* 37, no. 1 (October 1984): 1–23.

6. Quoted in Anthony Marro, "When the Government Tells Lies,"
Columbia Journalism Review 23, no. 6 (March/April 1985): 34. See
also Arthur Sylvester, "The Government Has the Right to Lie,"
Saturday Evening Post, November 18, 1967, 10, 14.

7. Jody Powell, *The Other Side of the Story* (New York: Morrow,
1984), 223. It should be noted, however, that Powell did not think
government leaders had to lie often—he only did it twice in his
four years in the White House—and he deeply regretted that it was
necessary on those occasions (ibid., 223–40).

8. Regarding the Rhineland, the historian Alan Bullock writes: "Years
later, reminiscing over the dinner table, Hitler asked: 'What would
have happened if anybody other than myself had been at the head
of the Reich! Anyone you care to mention would have lost his
nerve. I was obliged to lie and what saved me was my unshakeable
obstinacy and my amazing aplomb. I threatened unless the situation
eased to send six extra divisions into the Rhineland.The truth was,
I had only four brigades. Next day, the English papers wrote that
there had been an easing of the situation.'" Alan Bullock, *Hitler, a
Study in Tyranny,* rev. ed. (New York: Harper & Row, 1964), 343.
See also Michael Mihalka, *German Strategic Deception in the 1930s,*
Rand Note N-1557-NA (Santa Monica, CA: Rand Corporation,
July 1980); Arnd Plagge, "Patterns of Deception: Why and How
Rising States Cloak Their Power" (working paper, Yale University,
March 18, 2009).

9. Gorodetsky, *Grand Delusion,* 115–18, 126–30, 207–10; Jiri Hochman,
The Soviet Union and the Failure of Collective Security, 1934–1938
(Ithaca, NY: Cornell University Press, 1984), chap. 6; Adam B.
Ulam, *Expansion and Coexistence: Soviet Foreign Policy, 1917–73,*

2nd ed. (New York: Praeger, 1974), 241–43, 252–53; Adam B. Ulam, *Stalin: The Man and His Era* (New York: Viking, 1973), 502–3.

10. Edgar M. Bottome, *The Missile Gap: A Study of the Formulation of Military and Political Policy* (Rutherford, NJ: Farleigh Dickinson University Press, 1971), chaps. 2, 7; McGeorge Bundy, *Danger and Survival* (New York: Random House, 1988), 416; Arnold L. Horelick and Myron Rush, *Strategic Power and Soviet Foreign Policy* (Chicago: University of Chicago Press, 1966), chaps. 3–5, 9; Vladislav Zubok and Constantine Pleshakov, *Inside the Kremlin's Cold War: From Stalin to Khrushchev* (Cambridge, MA: Harvard University Press, 1996), chap. 6.

11. Holger H. Herwig, "The Failure of German Sea Power, 1914–1945: Mahan, Tirpitz, and Raeder Reconsidered," *International History Review* 10, no. 1 (February 1988): 68–105; Paul M. Kennedy, "Tirpitz, England and the Second Navy Law of 1900: A Strategical Critique," *Militärgeschichtliche Mitteilungen* 2 (1970): 33–57; Paul M. Kennedy, *The Rise of the Anglo-German Antagonism, 1860–1914* (London: Allen & Unwin, 1980), chap. 13, especially 223–27; Paul M. Kennedy, *Strategy and Diplomacy, 1870–1945: Eight Studies* (London: Fontana, 1984), chaps. 4–5; Jonathan Steinberg, *Yesterday's Deterrent: Tirpitz and the Birth of the German Battle Fleet* (London: Macdonald, 1965), intro., chaps. 4–5.

12. Quoted in "Report: Nixon Feared Israeli Nukes Would Spur Arms Race," *Haaretz,* November 29, 2007. See also Avner Cohen, *Israel and the Bomb* (New York: Columbia University Press, 1998); Seymour M. Hersh, *The Samson Option: Israel's Nuclear Arsenal and American Foreign Policy* (New York: Random House, 1991).

13. Bundy, *Danger and Survival,* 392. See also Graham Allison and Philip Zelikow, *Essence of Decision: Explaining the Cuban Missile Crisis,* 2nd ed. (New York: Longman, 1999), 78–80; Aleksandr Fursenko and Timothy Naftali, *One Hell of a Gamble: Khrushchev, Castro, and Kennedy, 1958–1964* (New York: Norton, 1997), 222–23, 252–53; Zubok and Pleshakov, *Inside the Kremlin's Cold War,* 266.

14. Trevor Wilson, *The Myriad Faces of War: Britain and the Great War, 1914–1918* (Cambridge, UK: Polity Press, 1988), 341; Ernest D. Swinton, *Eyewitness: Being Personal Reminiscences of Certain Phases of the Great War, Including the Genesis of the Tank* (Garden City, NY: Doubleday, Doran, 1933), chap. 12. See also B. H. Liddell Hart, *The Real War: 1914–1918* (Boston: Little, Brown, 1930), 249, 255;

B. H. Liddell Hart, *The Tanks: The History of the Royal Tank Regiment and Its Predecessors, Heavy Branch, Machine-Gun Corps, Tank Corps, and Royal Tank Corps, 1914–1945* (London: Cassell, 1959), 1:3, 1:47, 1:53–56.

15. Ken Alibek with Stephen Handelman, *Biohazard: The Chilling True Story of the Largest Covert Biological Weapons Program in the World, Told from the Inside by the Man Who Ran It* (New York: Dell, 2000); Jeanne Guillemin, *Anthrax: The Investigation of a Deadly Outbreak* (Berkeley: University of California Press, 1999); Matthew Meselson et al., "The Sverdlovsk Anthrax Outbreak of 1979," *Science,* November 18, 1994, 1202–8; Judith Miller, Stephen Engelberg, and William Broad, *Germs: Biological Weapons and America's Secret War* (New York: Simon and Schuster, 2001).

16. Quoted in Bullock, *Hitler,* 329. See also ibid., chap. 6; Ian Kershaw, *The "Hitler Myth": Image and Reality in the Third Reich* (New York: Oxford University Press, 1989), chap. 5; Ian Kershaw, *Hitler: 1889–1936; Hubris* (New York: Norton, 1999), chaps. 11–12; Ian Kershaw, *Hitler: 1936–45; Nemesis* (New York: Norton, 2000), chap. 1; Mihalka, "German Strategic Deception."

17. Quoted in Joachim C. Fest, *Hitler,* trans. Richard and Clara Winston (New York: Harcourt Brace Jovanovich, 1974), 556.

18. Tsuyoshi Hasegawa, *Racing the Enemy: Stalin, Truman, and the Surrender of Japan* (Cambridge, MA: Belknap Press of Harvard University Press, 2005), 108. See also 33, 39, 46–47, 56, 86, 91–93, 190–91.

19. Richard M. Nixon, *Six Crises* (Garden City, NY: Doubleday, 1962), 353–57; James P. Pfiffner, *The Character Factor: How We Judge America's Presidents* (College Station: Texas A & M University Press, 2004), 22, 24.

20. Powell, *Other Side of the Story,* 225–32.

21. Marc Trachtenberg, *A Constructed Peace: The Making of the European Settlement, 1945–1963* (Princeton, NJ: Princeton University Press, 1999), appendix 2, also available online at http://www.sscnet.ucla.edu/polisci/faculty/trachtenberg/appendices/appendixII.html

22. Norman Rich, *Friedrich von Holstein, Politics and Diplomacy in the Era of Bismarck and Wilhelm II* (Cambridge, UK: Cambridge University Press, 1965), 2:745. See also ibid., 2:678–745; David G. Herrmann, *The Arming of Europe and the Making of the First World War* (Princeton, NJ: Princeton University Press, 1996),

chap. 2; Gerhard Ritter, *The Schlieffen Plan: Critique of a Myth,*
trans. Andrew and Eva Wilson (Westport, CT: Greenwood, 1979),
96–128; L. C. F. Turner, *Origins of the First World War* (New York:
Norton, 1970), 2–5. It appears that the Moroccan Crisis is the
only known case of a country making an empty verbal threat for
coercive purposes. Glenn H. Snyder and Paul Diesing, *Conflict
among Nations: Bargaining, Decision Making, and System Structure
in International Crises* (Princeton, NJ: Princeton University Press,
1977), 213–16.

23. Bob Woodward, "Gadhafi Target of Secret U.S. Deception Plan,"
Washington Post, October 2, 1986. See also Gerald M. Boyd, "The
Administration Denies Planting Reports in the U.S.," *New York
Times,* October 3, 1986; Leslie H. Gelb, "Administration is Accused
of Deceiving Press on Libya," *New York Times,* October 3, 1986;
Alex S. Jones, "Initial Report on Libyan Plots Stirred Skepticism,"
New York Times, October 3, 1986; Jeffery T. Richelson, "Planning
to Deceive: How the Defense Department Practices the Fine Art
of Making Friends and Influencing People," *Bulletin of the Atomic
Scientists* 59, no. 2 (March/April 2003): 67–68.

24. After discussing the problems presented by strategic nuclear parity,
Henry Kissinger writes, "The answer of our NATO friends to
the situation I have described has invariably been to demand
additional reassurances of an undiminished American military
commitment. And I have sat around the NATO Council table
in Brussels and elsewhere and have uttered the magic words
which had a profoundly reassuring effect, and which permitted
the Ministers to return home with a rationale for not increasing
defense expenditures. And my successors have uttered the same
reassurances and yet if my analysis is correct these words cannot
be true, and if my analysis is correct we must face the fact that
it is absurd to base the strategy of the West on the credibility of
the threat of mutual suicide." "NATO: The Next Thirty Years,"
Atlantic Community Quarterly 17, no. 4 (Winter 1979/1980): 468.
See also Dana H. Allin, *Cold War Illusions: America, Europe, and Soviet
Power, 1969–1989* (New York: St. Martin's, 1994), chap. 4; Robert S.
McNamara, "The Military Role of Nuclear Weapons: Perceptions
and Misperceptions," *Foreign Affairs,* Fall 1983, 79.

25. William Carr, *The Origins of the Wars of German Unification* (London:
Longman, 1991), 144–203; F. Darmstaedter, *Bismarck and the Creation*

of the Second Reich (New York: Russell & Russell, 1965), 351–63; Lothar Gall, *Bismarck: The White Revolutionary,* trans. J. A. Underwood (Boston: Allen & Unwin, 1986), 1:346–59; W. N. Medlicott, *Bismarck and Modern Germany* (New York: Harper & Row, 1968), 78–84; Otto Pflanze, *Bismarck and the Development of Germany: The Period of Unification, 1815–1871* (Princeton, NJ: Princeton University Press, 1973), chap. 18.

26. Barbara Demick, "'Intelligence Fiasco' Stirs Up the Korean Peninsula," *Los Angeles Times,* March 24, 2005; Dafna Linzer, "U.S. Misled Allies about Nuclear Export," *Washington Post,* March 20, 2005.

27. Dwight D. Eisenhower, *Waging Peace, 1956–1961: The White House Years* (Garden City, NY: Doubleday, 1965), 546. See also James Bamford, *Body of Secrets: Anatomy of the Ultra-Secret National Security Agency; From the Cold War through the Dawn of a New Century* (New York: Doubleday, 2001); Michael R. Beschloss, *MAYDAY: Eisenhower, Khrushchev and the U-2 Affair* (New York: Harper & Row, 1986); Ted Galen Carpenter, *The Captive Press: Foreign Policy Crises and the First Amendment* (Washington, DC: Cato Institute, 1995), 55–56; David Wise and Thomas B. Ross, *The U-2 Affair* (New York: Random House, 1962).

28. Quoted in Benny Morris, *Righteous Victims: A History of the Zionist-Arab Conflict, 1881–1999* (New York: Knopf, 1999), 281–82. See also Joel Beinin, *The Dispersion Of Egyptian Jewry: Culture, Politics, And The Formation Of A Modern Diaspora* (Berkeley: University of California Press, 1998), 19–20, 31–32, 90–117; Dan Raviv and Yossi Melman, *Every Spy a Prince: The Complete History of Israel's Intelligence Community* (Boston: Houghton Mifflin, 1990), 54–61; Livia Rokach, *Israel's Sacred Terrorism: A Study Based on Moshe Sharett's Personal Diary and Other Documents,* 2nd ed. (Belmont, MA: Association of Arab-American University Graduates, 1982), 38–42; Shabtai Teveth, *Ben-Gurion's Spy: The Story of the Political Scandal That Shaped Modern Israel* (New York: Columbia University Press, 1996).

29. Quoted in Anthony Cave Brown, *Bodyguard of Lies* (New York: Harper & Row, 1975), 10. See also Thaddeus Holt, *The Deceivers: Allied Military Deception in the Second World War* (New York: Skyhorse, 2007); Phillip Knightley, *The First Casualty: From the Crimea to Vietnam; The War Correspondent as Hero, Propagandist, and*

Myth Maker (New York: Harcourt Brace Jovanovich, 1975); Michael Howard, *Strategic Deception in the Second World War* (New York: Norton, 1995); Harold D. Lasswell, *Propaganda Technique in the World War* (New York: Knopf, 1927); J. C. Masterman, *The Double-Cross System in the War of 1939 to 1945* (New Haven, CT: Yale University Press, 1972); Arthur Ponsonby, *Falsehood in War-Time, Containing an Assortment of Lies Circulated throughout the Nations during the Great War* (New York: Dutton, 1928); Evelin Sullivan, *The Concise Book of Lying* (New York: Farrar, Straus and Giroux, 2001), 229–53.

30. Quoted in Warren F. Kimball, *The Juggler: Franklin Roosevelt as Wartime Statesman* (Princeton, NJ: Princeton University Press, 1991), 7.

31. It is important to note that militaries place a high premium on truth telling within the organization, because it is an essential ingredient of success in combat. Everyone in the chain of command needs to be confident that they are receiving truthful information from their superiors and subordinates. Otherwise, commanders and their staffs would make plans and wage war on the basis of faulty information, which would markedly increase the likelihood of failure as well as unnecessary casualties. This is why institutions like West Point place great emphasis on their honor code. While deception has no place inside a military organization, it is expected that rival militaries will try to deceive each other, especially in wartime.

32. Thomas C. Schelling, *The Strategy of Conflict* (London: Oxford University Press, 1970), 23, 33. See also Thomas C. Schelling, "Game Theory and the Study of Ethical Systems," *Journal of Conflict Resolution* 12, no. 1 (March 1968): 34–44.

33. Although the conventional wisdom is that bluffing is commonplace in labor negotiations, at least one scholar argues that it happens "less often than many writers suggest." Chris Provis, "Ethics, Deception and Labor Negotiation," *Journal of Business Ethics* 28, no. 2 (November 2000): 145–58.

34. The same logic explains why poker players do not show their hole cards following a successful bluff; if they did, the tactic might not work again.

35. There is hardly any evidence of lying in Andrew Moravcsik's detailed analysis of the various bargains among the European countries that created the European Union, *The Choice for Europe: Social Purpose and State Power from Messina to Maastricht*

(Ithaca, NY: Cornell University Press, 1998). Although Moravcsik does not directly say why lying is absent from the history he examined, it seems clear that it is because he believes that the relevant European states only came to the bargaining table when: (1) there was substantial overlap among their preferences; (2) they all knew a great about "the range of potential agreements, national preferences, and institutional options"; and (3) they all thought that an agreement would lead to "joint gains." Not only would it have been hard to lie in such an information-rich environment, but it also would have made no sense, because such deceitful behavior probably would have scuttled the deal, "a result that would leave all worse off" (ibid., 61, 481–85).

36. Anthee Carassava, "Greece Admits Faking Data to Join Europe," *New York Times,* September 23, 2004; Daniel Howden and Stephen Castle, "Greece Admits Deficit Figures Were Fudged to Secure Euro Entry," *Independent,* November 16, 2004; Helena Smith and Larry Elliot, "EU Raps Greece over Deficit," *Guardian,* December 2, 2004.

37. Trachtenberg, *Constructed Peace,* 121–22. See also James McAllister, *No Exit: America and the German Problem, 1943–1954* (Ithaca, NY: Cornell University Press, 2002), 225.

38. McCallister, *No Exit,* 234. See also minutes of National Security Council Meeting, December 10, 1953, in *Foreign Relations of the United States, 1952–1954* (Washington, DC: Government Printing Office, 1983), 2:450–51.

39. Ponsonby, *Falsehood in War-Time,* 19.

40. Charles Horton Cooley, *Human Nature and the Social Order,* rev. ed. (New York: Scribner's Sons, 1922), 388.

Chapter 4

1. James Chace, *Acheson: The Secretary of State Who Created the American World* (New York: Simon and Schuster, 1998), chap. 16.

2. Quoted in Michael Hirsh, "Bernard Lewis Revisited," *Washington Monthly,* November 2004.

3. Among the best sources on the *Greer* incident are Robert Dallek, *Franklin D. Roosevelt and American Foreign Policy, 1932–1945* (New York: Oxford University Press, 1979), 285–88; Waldo Heinrichs, *Threshold of War: Franklin D. Roosevelt and American Entry into World War II* (New York: Oxford University Press, 1989), 166–68;

David M. Kennedy, *Freedom from Fear: The American People in Depression and War, 1929–1945* (New York: Oxford University Press, 1999), 497–99; William L. Langer and S. Everett Gleason, *The Undeclared War: 1940–1941* (Gloucester, MA: Smith, 1968), 742–50; David Reynolds, *The Creation of the Anglo-American Alliance, 1937–41: A Study in Competitive Co-operation* (Chapel Hill: University of North Carolina Press, 1982), chap. 8; John M. Schuessler, "The Deception Dividend: FDR's Undeclared War," *International Security* 34, no. 4 (Spring 2010): 133–65

4. As Robert Divine notes, "The submarine commander, far from being guilty of an unprovoked assault, had turned in desperation on his pursuer in an effort to escape destruction." *The Reluctant Belligerent: American Entry into World War II* (New York: Wiley, 1967), 143.

5. All the quotations in this paragraph and the next are from Dallek, *Roosevelt and American Foreign Policy,* 285–88; see also Langer and Gleason, *Undeclared War,* 744–46.

6. Among the best sources on the Gulf of Tonkin incident are: Eric Alterman, *When Presidents Lie: A History of Official Deception and Its Consequences* (New York: Viking, 2004), chap. 4; Joseph C. Goulden, *Truth Is the First Casualty: The Gulf of Tonkin Affair; Illusion and Reality* (Chicago: Rand McNally, 1969); Robert J. Hanyok, "Skunks, Bogies, Silent Hounds, and the Flying Fish: The Gulf of Tonkin Mystery, 2–4 August 1964," *Cryptologic Quarterly* 19 and 20, nos. 4 and 1 (Winter 2000 and Spring 2001), 1–55; David Kaiser, *American Tragedy: Kennedy, Johnson, and the Origins of the Vietnam War* (Cambridge, MA: Belknap Press of Harvard University Press, 2000), chap. 11; Fredrik Logevall, *Choosing War: The Lost Chance for Peace and the Escalation of War in Vietnam* (Berkeley: University of California Press, 1999), chap. 7; H. R. McMaster, *Dereliction of Duty: Lyndon Johnson, Robert McNamara, the Joint Chiefs of Staff, and the Lies That Led to Vietnam* (New York: HarperCollins, 1997), chap. 6; Edwin E. Moïse, *Tonkin Gulf and the Escalation of the Vietnam War* (Chapel Hill: University of North Carolina Press, 1996); Gareth Porter, *Perils of Dominance: Imbalance of Power and the Road to War in Vietnam* (Berkeley: University of California Press, 2005), chap. 6.

7. Alterman, *When Presidents Lie,* 204–5.

8. Alterman, *When Presidents Lie,* 193. These are Alterman's words.

9. Goulden, *First Casualty,* 50.

10. Hanyok, "Skunks," 21–49; Moïse, *Tonkin Gulf,* 206–10, 241–43. See also Alterman, *When Presidents Lie,* 186–90.

11. Logevall, *Choosing War*, 198. These are Logevall's words. See also Porter, *Perils of Dominance*, 196–98.

12. Kaiser, *American Tragedy*, 335–36.

13. Moïse, *Tonkin Gulf*, 243. These are Moïse's words. It is now clear that there was no attack on the *Maddox* on August 4, 1964. Hanyok, "Skunks," 3.

14. Moïse, *Tonkin Gulf*, 243.

15. These were the words used by McNamara and Secretary of State Dean Rusk when testifying before the House Foreign Affairs Committee on August 6. Logevall, *Choosing War*, 203. See also ibid., 198–99; and McMaster, *Dereliction of Duty*, 133–35, for similar comments by President Johnson and other senior administration officials.

16. Michael R. Beschloss, *Taking Charge: The Johnson White House Tapes, 1963–1964* (New York: Simon and Schuster, 1997), 494–95; Hanyok, "Skunks," 5–12; Logevall, *Choosing War*, 201; McMaster, *Dereliction of Duty*, 121–30; Moïse, *Tonkin Gulf*, 99–105, 228–29, 239–41.

17. See Logevall, *Choosing War*, 199–203; Moïse, *Tonkin Gulf*, 99–105.

18. Alterman, *When Presidents Lie*, 205; Logevall, *Choosing War*, 203. One might argue that the Johnson administration told a third lie related to the Gulf of Tonkin incident. The president and his chief advisors claimed throughout 1964 and into early 1965 that they had no intention, much less plans, for escalating the war in Vietnam. In fact, Johnson portrayed himself as the peace candidate in his 1964 campaign for the presidency against Barry Goldwater. However, throughout that period, Johnson was actually laying the plans for expanding the war, as is evidenced by his behavior in the Gulf of Tonkin incident. For further elaboration on this matter, see Alterman, *When Presidents Lie*, chap. 4; Kaiser, *American Tragedy*, chap. 11; Logevall, *Choosing War*, 193–221, 242, 253, 314–15; Deborah Shapley, *Promise and Power: The Life and Times of Robert McNamara* (Boston: Little, Brown, 1993), 304–5.

19. Eric Schmitt, "Rumsfeld Says U.S. Has 'Bulletproof' Evidence of Iraq's Links to Al Qaeda," *New York Times*, September 28, 2002.

20. Thom Shanker, "Rumsfeld Sees Lack of Proof for Qaeda-Hussein Link," *New York Times*, October 5, 2004.

21. The Powell quotes are from Richard Cohen, "Powellian Propaganda?" *Washington Post*, February 13, 2003; *Iraq on the Record: The Bush Administration's Public Statements on Iraq*, Report prepared for Congressman Henry A. Waxman by the Minority

Staff, Committee on Government Reform, U.S. House of Representatives, March 16, 2004, 23; Transcript of Secretary Powell's Press Conference, January 8, 2004. See also Derrick Z. Jackson, "Powell's Shrinking Credibility on Iraq," *Boston Globe,* January 14, 2004; Christopher Marquis, "Powell Admits No Hard Proof in Linking Iraq to Al Qaeda," *New York Times,* January 9, 2004.

22. Spencer Ackerman and John Judis, "Deception and Democracy: The Selling of the Iraq War," *New Republic,* June 30, 2003, 18; Douglas Jehl, "Report Warned Bush Team about Intelligence Doubts," *New York Times,* November 6, 2005; Mark Mazzetti, "C.I.A. Said to Find No Hussein Link to Terror Chief," *New York Times,* September 9, 2006; John Prados, "Phase II: Loaded for Bear," *TomPaine.com,* November 10, 2005; Senate Select Committee on Intelligence, *Postwar Findings about Iraq's WMD Programs and Links to Terrorism and How They Compare with Prewar Assessments,* 109th Cong., 2d sess., September 8, 2006, 60–112; Jonathan Weisman, "Iraq's Alleged Al-Qaeda Ties Were Disputed Before War," *Washington Post,* September 9, 2006.

23. Walter Pincus and Dana Milbank, "Al Qaeda–Hussein Link Is Dismissed," *Washington Post,* June 17, 2004.

24. Bob Woodward, *Plan of Attack* (New York: Simon and Schuster, 2004), 173.

25. For example, George Tenet, the head of the CIA in the run-up to the war, said in a speech on February 5, 2004: "We believe[d] that Iraq had lethal biological agents, including anthrax, which it could quickly produce and weaponize for delivery by bombs, missiles, aerial sprayers and covert operatives. But we said we had no specific information on the types or quantities of weapons, agent or stockpiles at Baghdad's disposal." For a transcript of the speech, see "Tenet Defends Assessments of Iraqi Weapons," *New York Times,* February 5, 2004. The Defense Intelligence Agency reported in September 2002 that there was no "hard" or "direct" evidence of chemical and biological stockpiles or production facilities. See Joseph Cirincione's comments in *Conference Call Briefing on Iraq's Weapons* (Washington, DC: Arms Control Association, February 3, 2004). See also *Iraq on the Record,* 15–16; Walter Pincus and Dana Priest, "Bush, Aides Ignored CIA Caveats on Iraq," *Washington Post,* February 7, 2004; Senate Select Committee on Intelligence, *Postwar Findings about Iraq's WMD Programs,* 26–43.

26. *Iraq on the Record,* 7.

27. Jackson, "Powell's Shrinking Credibility."

28. See Joseph Cirincione, Jessica Tuchman Mathews, and George Perkovich, *WMD in Iraq: Evidence and Implications* (Carnegie Endowment Report, January 2004), 86, http://carnegieendowment.org/files/Iraq3FullText.pdf.

29. Ibid., 18, 95.

30. Ibid., *WMD in Iraq,* 20; *Iraq on the Record,* 16.

31. Cirincione, Mathews, and Perkovich, *WMD in Iraq,* 21.

32. See Pincus and Priest, "Bush, Aides Ignored CIA Caveats"; *Iraq on the Record,* 10–13; Senate Select Committee on Intelligence, *Postwar Findings about Iraq's WMD Programs,* 17–21; Murray Waas, "What Bush Was Told about Iraq," *National Journal,* March 2, 2006.

33. See Ackerman and Judis, "Deception and Democracy," 15; Cirincione, Mathews, and Perkovich, *WMD in Iraq,* 21–28; Senate Select Committee on Intelligence, *Postwar Findings about Iraq's WMD Programs,* 10–26; "Tenet Defends Assessments of Iraqi Weapons"; Greg Thielman's comments in "Conference Call Briefing on Iraq's Weapons"; *Iraq on the Record,* 7–15.

34. See Ronald Brownstein, "Support of U.S. Military Role in Mideast Grows," *Los Angeles Times,* April 5, 2003; The Gallup Organization, *Approval for Handling of War in Iraq Jumps,* Poll Analysis, December 19, 2003; Adam Nagourney and Janet Elder, "Growing Number in U.S. Back War, Survey Finds," *New York Times,* March 11, 2003; Tom Zeller, "The Iraq-Qaeda Link: A Short History," *New York Times,* June 20, 2004; Tom Zeller, "Making a Simple Link of Faith," *New York Times,* March 2, 2003. At least one reputable polling organization found in September 2003, two years after the Twin Towers fell and almost six months after the start of the Iraq war, that "seven in ten Americans continue to believe that Iraq's Saddam Hussein had a role in the attacks." See Dana Milbank and Claudia Deane, "Hussein Link to 9/11 Lingers in Many Minds," *Washington Post,* September 6, 2003.

35. See "Cheney: No Link between Saddam Hussein, 9/11," *CNN.com,* June 1, 2009, http://www.cnn.com/2009/POLITICS/06/01/cheney.speech/; Rebecca Christie, "US Rumsfeld Concedes No WMDs or September 11 Ties in Iraq," *Dow Jones Newswires,* September 17, 2004; Cirincione, Mathews, and Perkovich, *WMD in Iraq,* 44; Milbank and Deane, "Hussein Link to 9/11 Lingers";

Greg Miller, "No Proof Connects Iraq to 9/11, Bush Says," *Los Angeles Times,* September 18, 2003; Paul Reynolds, "Rumsfeld Weakens a Pillar of War," *BBC News Online,* October 5, 2004, http://news.bbc.co.uk/2/hi/americas/3717024.stm; David E. Sanger, "Bush Reports No Evidence of Hussein Tie to 9/11," *New York Times,* September 18, 2003; Susan Walsh, "Rumsfeld Sees No Link between Saddam Hussein, 9/11," *USA Today,* September 16, 2003. An article in the *National Journal* reports that "ten days after the September 11, 2001, terrorist attacks on the World Trade Center and the Pentagon, President Bush was told in a highly classified briefing that the U.S. intelligence community had no evidence linking the Iraqi regime of Saddam Hussein to the attacks and that there was scant credible evidence that Iraq had any significant collaborative ties with Al Qaeda, according to government records and current and former officials with firsthand knowledge of the matter." Murray Waas, "Key Bush Intelligence Briefing Kept from Hill Panel," *National Journal,* November 22, 2005.

36. Transcript of testimony of U.S. Secretary of Defense Donald H. Rumsfeld before the Senate Armed Services Committee Regarding Iraq, September 19, 2002.

37. Letter from the President to the Speaker of the House of Representatives and the President Pro Tempore of the Senate, March 18, 2003.

38. "Bush Makes Historic Speech aboard Warship," *CNN.com,* May 1, 2003, http://www.cnn.com/2003/US/05/01/bush.transcript/. See also Jim Rutenberg and Sheryl Gay Stolberg, "Bush Says G.O.P. Rebels are Putting Nation at Risk," *New York Times,* September 16, 2006; David E. Sanger and Robin Toner, "Bush and Cheney Talk Strongly of Qaeda Links with Hussein," *New York Times,* June 18, 2004.

39. *New York Times,* "What the Bush Administration Said," June 20, 2004; Christopher Scheer, Robert Scheer, and Lakshmi Chaudhry, *The Five Biggest Lies Bush Told Us About Iraq* (New York: Seven Stories, 2003), 42.

40. Another lie that served the same purpose was President Bush's claim—which he made on three separate occasions—that Saddam Hussein refused to allow UN inspectors into Iraq in late 2002, and therefore he had no choice but to remove the Iraqi leader from power. Joe Conason, "Saddam Chose to Deny Inspectors," *Salon,* March 31, 2006, http://www.salon.com/news/opinion/

joe_conason/2006/03/31/bush_lies. Of course, Saddam allowed the inspectors into Iraq and gave them free reign to look for WMD. However, Bush pulled them out before they finished the job, and then invaded Iraq. For an excellent overview of the Bush administration's deception campaign in the run-up to the Iraq war, see David Corn, "Can the 'Bush Lied' Deniers Handle the Truth?" *Politics Daily,* March 17, 2010, http://www.politicsdaily. com/2010/03/17/can-the-bush-lied-deniers-handle-the-truth/; David Corn, "Charges and Countercharges: Did Bush Knowingly Mislead the U.S. into War with Iraq?" *Politics Daily,* March 30, 2010, http://www.politicsdaily.com/2010/03/30/a-long-war-did-bush-knowingly-mislead-the-u-s-into-iraq/.

41. Woodward, *Plan of Attack,* 296; Brian Knowlton, "Diplomacy Won't Be Given 'Months,'" *New York Times,* January 31, 2003. See also Bush's comments in Scheer, Scheer, and Chaudhry, *Five Biggest Lies,* 80.

42. Scheer, Scheer, and Chaudhry, *Five Biggest Lies,* 80.

43. Nicholas Lemann, "How It Came to War; When Did Bush Decide That He Had to Fight Saddam?" *New Yorker,* March 31, 2003. See also Richard N. Haass, *War of Necessity, War of Choice: A Memoir of Two Iraq Wars* (New York: Simon and Schuster, 2009), 4–6.

44. *Times* (London), "The Secret Downing Street Memo," May 1, 2005. See also Michael Smith, "The Real News in the Downing Street Memos," *Los Angeles Times,* June 23, 2005.

45. Woodward, *Plan of Attack,* 269–74. For other evidence that Bush had decided to go to war before the end of January, 2003, see ibid., 95, 113, 115, 119–20, 169, 178. Also, there was evidence in the media during 2002 that the Bush administration had decided to remove Saddam by force. For example, see John Walcott and Mark Danner, "The Secret Way to War: An Exchange," *New York Review of Books,* July 14, 2005, 48–49.

46. Note that in this instance the Bush administration was engaging in both fearmongering and inter-state lying, which reminds us that a particular lie can be directed at multiple audiences and serve multiple purposes.

47. For an excellent discussion of why and how leaders inflate threats, see A. Trevor Thrall and Jane K. Cramer, eds., *American Foreign Policy and the Politics of Fear: Threat Inflation since 9/11* (New York: Routledge, 2009).

48. Steven Casey, "Selling NSC-68: The Truman Administration, Public Opinion, and the Politics of Mobilization, 1950–51," *Diplomatic History* 29, no. 4 (September 2005): 655–90. In fact, the Truman administration's rhetoric was so alarmist that there was "a very real fear that the popular mood could easily overheat, thereby reducing officials' freedom to maneuver and perhaps even pushing them toward excessively radical and dangerous policies" (ibid., 661). See also Nancy E. Bernhard, *U.S. Television News and Cold War Propaganda, 1947–1960* (New York: Cambridge University Press, 1999); Campbell Craig and Fredrik Logevall, *America's Cold War: The Politics of Insecurity* (Cambridge, MA: Belknap Press of Harvard University Press, 2009).

49. Leslie Gelb with Jeanne-Paloma Zelmati, "Mission Unaccomplished," *Democracy,* no. 13 (Summer 2009): 24.

50. The classic brief against the Articles of Confederation is Alexander Hamilton, James Madison, and John Jay, *The Federalist Papers,* ed. Isaac Kramnick (Harmondsworth, UK: Penguin Books, 1987), 145–84. For critiques of American policy-making machinery under the Constitution, see Theodore J. Lowi, "Making Democracy Safe for the World: National Politics and Foreign Policy," in James N. Rosenau, ed., *Domestic Sources of Foreign Policy* (New York: Free Press, 1967), 295–331; Theodore J. Lowi, *The End of Liberalism: The Second Republic of the United States,* 2nd ed. (New York: Norton, 1979); E. E. Schattschneider, *The Semisovereign People: A Realist's View of Democracy in America* (Fort Worth, TX: Harcourt Brace Jovanovich, 1975). See also Michel Crozier, Samuel P. Huntington, and Joji Watanuki, *The Crisis of Democracy: Report on the Governability of Democracies to the Trilateral Commission,* Triangle Papers 8 (New York: New York University Press, 1975); and David Donald's essay, "Died of Democracy," in David Donald, ed., *Why the North Won the Civil War* (New York: Collier Books, 1962), 79–90, in which he argues that the South lost the Civil War because it was too democratic.

51. Alterman, *When Presidents Lie,* 210.

52. Richard Cohen, "A War without Winners," *Washington Post,* November 3, 2005.

53. James Burnham, *Suicide of the West: An Essay on the Meaning and Destiny of Liberalism* (New Rochelle, NY: Arlington House, 1964); Donald Kagan and Fredrick W. Kagan, *While America Sleeps:*

Self-Delusion, Military Weakness, and the Threat to Peace Today (New York: St. Martin's, 2000); Donald Kagan, *On the Origins of War and the Preservation of Peace* (New York: Doubleday, 1995), 572–73; Robert G. Kaufman, "To Balance or to Bandwagon? Alignment Decisions in 1930s Europe," *Security Studies* 1, no. 3 (Spring 1992): 417–47; Norman Podhoretz, *The Present Danger: Do We Have the Will to Reverse the Decline of American Power?* (New York: Simon and Schuster, 1980); Jean-François Revel, *How Democracies Perish,* trans. William Byron (Garden City, NY: Doubleday, 1984).

54. Quoted in Ronald Bailey, "Origins of the Specious: Why Do Neoconservatives Doubt Darwin?" *Reason,* July 1997.

55. Walter Lippmann, "Why Should the Majority Rule?" in Clinton Rossiter and James Lare, eds., *The Essential Lippmann: A Political Philosophy for Liberal Democracy* (New York: Random House, 1963), 6–14; Walter Lippmann, *The Phantom Public* (New York: Macmillan, 1927); Walter Lippmann, *Public Opinion* (New York: Free Press, 1965).

56. Ian Kershaw, *The "Hitler Myth": Image and Reality in the Third Reich* (New York: Oxford University Press, 1989), 3.

57. Great powers that act as offshore balancers are invariably "insular states" as opposed to "continental states." See John J. Mearsheimer, *The Tragedy of Great Power Politics* (New York: Norton, 2001), 126–28. On the "stopping power of water," see ibid., 114–28.

58. Michael Walzer, *Just and Unjust Wars: A Moral Argument with Historical Illustrations,* 3rd ed. (New York: Basic Books, 2000), 74–85. As John Schuessler notes, the incentives for leaders to deceive their public will be even greater if they anticipate that the preventive war will be long and bloody ("The Deception Dividend," 135–142). Of course, the Bush administration expected a quick and easy victory in Iraq.

59. The Bush Doctrine, which was laid out in 2002 and which provided the rationalization for invading Iraq, made the case for fighting preemptive wars against gathering threats, when, in fact, the Bush administration was contemplating preventive wars against Iraq and other countries in the Middle East. See *The National Security Strategy of the United States of America* (Washington, DC: White House, September 2002); Remarks by the President to the Graduating Class, West Point (White House, Office of the Press Secretary, June 1, 2002).

Chapter 5

1. Ian Ousby, *The Road to Verdun: World War I's Most Momentous Battle and the Folly of Nationalism* (New York: Anchor Books, 2003), 299. See also *New York Times,* "French Army Chief May Go," December 7, 1916; Robert A. Doughty, *Pyrrhic Victory: French Strategy and Operations in the Great War* (Cambridge, MA: Belknap Press of Harvard University Press, 2005), chaps. 5–6; Walter Duranty, "Joffre-Gallieni Dispute Bared, *New York Times,* August 21, 1919; Walter Duranty, "Joffre Ousted by Intrigues," *New York Times,* August 23, 1919; David Dutton, "The Fall of General Joffre: An Episode in the Politico-Military Struggle in Wartime France," *Journal of Strategic Studies* 19, no. 3 (December 1978): 338–51; Jere Clemens King, *Generals & Politicians: Conflict Between France's High Command, Parliament, and Government, 1914–1918* (Berkeley: University of California Press, 1951), chaps. 5–6; Harold D. Lasswell, *Propaganda Technique in the World War* (New York: Knopf, 1927), 39–40; Walter Lippmann, *Public Opinion* (New York: Free Press, 1965), chaps. 1–2; David Mason, *verdun* (Moreton-in-Marsh, UK: Windrush, 2000), 9–12, 23–27, 133–37, 182, 190–91; Gordon Wright, *Raymond Poincaré and the French Presidency* (Stanford, CA: Stanford University Press, 1942), 193–98.

2. Michael Bar-Zohar, *Ben-Gurion: A Biography,* trans. Peretz Kidron (New York: Delacorte, 1978), 203–6; Benny Morris, *Israel's Border Wars, 1949–1956: Arab Infiltration, Israeli Retaliation, and the Countdown to the Suez War,* rev. ed. (Oxford: Clarendon Press, 1997), chap. 8; Benny Morris, *Righteous Victims: A History of the Zionist-Arab Conflict, 1881–1999* (New York: Knopf, 1999), 278–79; Avi Shlaim, *The Iron Wall: Israel and the Arab World* (New York: Norton, 2000), 90–93.

3. Quoted in Morris, *Israel's Border Wars,* 259.

4. Shlaim, *Iron Wall,* 91.

5. Bar-Zohar, *Ben-Gurion,* 205.

6. Morris, *Righteous Victims,* 278–79.

7. Graham Allison and Philip Zelikow, *Essence of Decision: Explaining the Cuban Missile Crisis,* 2nd ed. (New York: Longman, 1999), 356–66; McGeorge Bundy, *Danger and Survival* (New York: Random House, 1988), 427–39, 445; Michael Dobbs, *One Minute to Midnight: Kennedy, Khrushchev, and Castro on the Brink of Nuclear War* (New York: Knopf, 2008), 199–201, 231–36, 257, 270–71,

288–93, 305–38 Aleksandr Fursenko and Timothy Naftali, *One Hell of a Gamble: Khrushchev, Castro, and Kennedy, 1958–1964* (New York: Norton, 1997), 249–50, 266–67, 275–89, 293–94, 300, 321–24, 352.

8. E. H. Carr, *German-Soviet Relations between the Two World Wars, 1919–1939* (Baltimore: Johns Hopkins Press, 1951), chaps. 3–4; Hans W. Gatzke, *Stresemann and the Rearmament of Germany* (New York: Norton, 1969), chaps. 4–5; George W. F. Hallgarten, "General Hans von Seeckt and Russia, 1920–1922," *Journal of Modern History* 21, no. 1 (March 1949): 28–34; Gustav Hilger and Alfred G. Meyer, *The Incompatible Allies: A Memoir-History of German-Soviet Relations, 1918–1941* (New York: Macmillan, 1953); Vasilis Vourkoutiotis, *Making Common Cause: German-Soviet Relations, 1919–22* (New York: Palgrave Macmillan, 2007).

9. Caroline Elkins, *Imperial Reckoning: The Untold Story of Britain's Gulag in Kenya* (New York: Holt, 2005), chaps. 9–10.

10. Martin Fackler, "Japanese Split on Exposing Secret Pacts with U.S.," *New York Times,* February 9, 2010; John M. Glionna, "Japan's Secret Pact with U.S. Spurs Debate," *Los Angeles Times,* January 17, 2010; Robert A. Wampler, ed., "Nuclear Noh Drama: Tokyo, Washington and the Case of the Missing Nuclear Agreements," *The National Security Archive,* October 13, 2009, http://www.gwu.edu/~nsarchiv/nukevault/ebb291/index.htm.

11. One might argue that masking incompetence is more likely in a democracy, because leaders are accountable to their people, who will punish them if they find out about their ineptitude. While I believe this is true, lying of this sort is done for selfish purposes, not for the good of the country. In other words, it would be an ignoble cover-up, not a strategic cover-up; as emphasized earlier, the former kind of lie falls outside the scope of this book. One might also argue the opposite: there is likely to be less need to hide mistakes in democracies, because democracies do a better job of making strategic choices than nondemocracies. See David A. Lake, "Powerful Pacifists: Democratic States and War," *American Political Science Review* 86, no. 1 (March 1992): 24–37; Dan Reiter and Allan C. Stam, *Democracies at War* (Princeton, NJ: Princeton University Press, 2002). However, a careful review of the logic and the evidence behind this claim shows that there is no meaningful difference in the ability of democracies and nondemocracies to make intelligent decisions in the foreign-policy realm.

See Michael C. Desch, *Power and Military Effectiveness: The Fallacy of Democratic Triumphalism* (Baltimore: Johns Hopkins University Press, 2008); Alexander B. Downes, "How Smart and Tough Are Democracies? Reassessing Theories of Democratic Victory in War," *International Security* 33, no. 4 (Spring 2009): 9–51; Sebastian Rosato, "The Flawed Logic of Democratic Peace Theory," *American Political Science Review* 97, no. 4 (November 2003): 585–602.

Chapter 6

1. This is not to say that a country's master narrative about its past is simply comprised of myths; it may also contain some truthful stories.

2. Stephen Van Evera, "Hypotheses on Nationalism and War," *International Security* 18, no. 4 (Spring 1994): 27.

3. Ernest Renan, "What Is a Nation?" in Geoff Eley and Ronald Grigor Suny, eds., *Becoming National: A Reader* (New York: Oxford University Press, 1996), 45.

4. Dominique Moisi, "France Is Haunted by an Inability to Confront its Past," *Financial Times,* December 12, 2005.

5. Van Evera notes that "nationalist myths can help politically frail elites to bolster their grip on power," and they can "bolster the authority and political power of incumbent elites" ("Hypotheses on Nationalism and War," 30). While this is certainly true, selfish lies of this sort fall outside the scope of this book.

6. The best book on this subject is Ronald Smelser and Edward J. Davies II, *The Myth of the Eastern Front: The Nazi-Soviet War in American Popular Culture* (New York: Cambridge University Press, 2008). See also Omer Bartov, *Germany's War and the Holocaust: Disputed Histories* (Ithaca, NY: Cornell University Press, 2003); Paula Bradish, *Crimes of the German Wehrmacht: Dimensions of a War of Annihilation, 1941–1944,* exhibition brochure (Hamburg, Germany: Hamburg Institute for Social Research, 2004); Norbert Frei, *Adenauer's Germany and the Nazi Past: The Politics of Amnesty and Intergration,* trans. Joel Golb (New York: Columbia University Press, 2002); Hannes Heer and Klaus Naumann, eds., *War of Extermination: The German Military in World War II, 1941–1944* (New York: Berghahn Books, 2000); John J. Mearsheimer, *Liddell Hart and the Weight of History* (Ithaca, NY: Cornell University Press, 1988), 178–201; Alaric Searle, *Wehrmacht Generals, West German Society,*

and the Debate on Rearmament, 1949–1959 (Westport, CT: Praeger, 2003); Wolfram Wette, *The Wehrmacht: History, Myth, Reality,* trans. Deborah Lucas Schneider (Cambridge, MA: Harvard University Press, 2006), chap. 5.

7. Christopher Simpson, *Blowback: America's Recruitment of Nazis and Its Effects on the Cold War* (New York: Collier Books, 1989), 158.

8. On the myth about why the Palestinians fled their homes, see Erskine Childers, "The Other Exodus," *Spectator,* May 12, 1961; Simha Flapan, *The Birth of Israel: Myths and Realities* (New York: Pantheon Books, 1987), 81–118; Walid Khalidi, "Why Did the Palestinians Leave, Revisited," *Journal of Palestine Studies* 34, no. 2 (Winter 2005): 42–54; Walid Khalidi, "The Fall of Haifa," *Middle East Forum* 35, no. 10 (December 1959): 22–32; Benny Morris, *The Birth of the Palestinian Refugee Problem Revisited,* 2nd ed. (New York: Cambridge University Press, 2004); Ilan Pappe, *The Ethnic Cleansing of Palestine* (Oxford: Oneworld, 2006), 131. For analysis of other myths, see Flapan, *Birth of Israel;* Norman G. Finkelstein, *Image and Reality of the Israel-Palestine Conflict* (London: Verso, 1995); John J. Mearsheimer and Stephen M. Walt, *The Israel Lobby and U.S. Foreign Policy* (New York: Farrar, Straus and Giroux, 2007), chap. 3; Benny Morris, *Righteous Victims: A History of the Zionist-Arab Conflict, 1881–1999* (New York: Knopf, 1999); Tom Segev, *One Palestine, Complete: Jews and Arabs under the British Mandate,* trans. Haim Watzman (New York: Holt, 2001); Avi Shlaim, *The Iron Wall: Israel and the Arab World* (New York: Norton, 2000); Zeev Sternhell, *The Founding Myths of Israel: Nationalism, Socialism, and the Making of the Jewish State,* trans. David Maisel (Princeton, NJ: Princeton University Press, 1998).

9. Van Evera, "Hypotheses on Nationalism and War," 29.

Chapter 7

1. Alexander B. Downes, *Targeting Civilians in War* (Ithaca, NY: Cornell University Press, 2008), 3.

2. Robert A. Pape, *Bombing to Win: Air Power and Coercion in War* (Ithaca, NY: Cornell University Press, 1996), chap. 4.

3. Quoted in Tim Weiner, "Robert S. McNamara, Architect of Futile War, Dies at 93," *New York Times,* July 6, 2009.

4. UNICEF, "Iraq Surveys Show 'Humanitarian Emergency,'" *Information Newsline,* August 12, 1999, http://www.unicef.org/newsline/99pr29.htm; Biswajit Sen, *Iraq Watching Briefs: Overview*

Report, UNICEF, July 2003, http://www.unicef.org/evaldatabase/
files/Iraq_2003_Watching_Briefs.pdf. Some argue that 500,000
deaths is too high a number. See, for examples, David Cortright,
"A Hard Look at Iraq Sanctions," *Nation,* December 3, 2001;
Matt Welch, "The Politics of Dead Children," *Reason,* March
2002, http://reason.com/archives/2002/03/01/the-politics-of-
dead-children. Whatever the exact number, David Rieff is almost
certainly right when he writes, "American officials may quarrel
with the numbers, but there is little doubt that at least several
hundred thousand children who could reasonably have been
expected to live died before their fifth birthdays" ("Were Sanctions
Right?" *New York Times Magazine,* July 27, 2003).

5. Benjamin A. Valentino, *Final Solutions: Mass Killings and Genocide
   in the Twentieth Century* (Ithaca, NY: Cornell University Press,
   2004), 73–75, 91–117. In his discussion of Hitler's murderous role
   in the Holocaust, Valentino notes: "If even a fraction of those who
   perished in the massive famines under Stalin and Mao are included,
   each of those tyrants is responsible for a greater absolute toll than
   Hitler, perhaps several times higher" (ibid., 177–78).

6. P. M. H. Bell, *John Bull and the Bear: British Public Opinion, Foreign
   Policy, and the Soviet Union, 1941–1945* (London: Arnold, 1990);
   Martin H. Folly, *Churchill, Whitehall, and the Soviet Union, 1940–45*
   (New York: St. Martin's, 2000); John Lewis Gaddis, *The United States
   and the Origins of the Cold War, 1941–1947* (New York: Columbia
   University Press, 1972), chap. 2; Ralph B. Levering, *American
   Opinion and the Russian Alliance, 1939–1945* (Chapel Hill: University
   of North Carolina Press, 1976), chaps. 3–5; Ido Oren, "The
   Subjectivity of the 'Democratic' Peace: Changing U.S. Perceptions
   of Imperial Germany," *International Security* 20, no. 2 (Fall 1995):
   181–82; Ronald Smelser and Edward J. Davies II, *The Myth of the
   Eastern Front: The Nazi-Soviet War in American Popular Culture*
   (New York: Cambridge University Press, 2008), chap. 1.

7. The Soviet Union murdered about 22,000 Poles in April–May
   1940. Roughly 4,400 were buried in the Katyn Forest. The
   remaining victims were killed and buried in other locations.
   George Sanford, *Katyn and the Soviet Massacre of 1940: Truth, Justice
   and Memory* (New York: Routledge, 2005), 1. Among the best
   sources on Katyn and how Churchill and Roosevelt reacted are
   Bell, *John Bull,* chap. 4; Allen Paul, *Katyń: The Untold Story of Stalin's*

Polish Massacre (New York: Scribner's, 1991), chap. 22; Sanford, *Katyn and the Soviet Massacre,* chaps. 6–7; Victor Zaslavsky, *Class Cleansing: The Katyn Massacre,* trans. Kizer Walker (New York: Telos, 2008), chap. 5.

8. Quoted in Paul, *Katyń,* 303.

9. Bell, *John Bull,* 119. On the Roosevelt administration's efforts to cover up Soviet responsibility for what happened in the Katyn forest, see Paul, *Katyń,* 306–15; Sanford, *Katyn and the Soviet Massacre,* 159–66.

10. The quotes in this paragraph are from Alan Bullock, *Hitler, a Study in Tyranny,* rev. ed. (New York: Harper & Row, 1964), 546–47. See also Joachim C. Fest, *Hitler,* trans. Richard and Clara Winston (New York: Harcourt Brace Jovanovich, 1974), 598–600; Bradley Lightbody, *The Second World War: Ambitions to Nemesis* (New York: Routledge, 2004), 39.

11. Max Hastings, *Bomber Campaign: Churchill's Epic Campaign* (New York: Simon and Schuster, 1989), 171. See also Stephen A. Garrett, *Ethics and Airpower in World War II: The British Bombing of German Cities* (New York: St. Martin's, 1993), 30–37.

12. David Bamber, "Bin Laden: Yes, I Did It," *Daily Telegraph,* November 11, 2001; Peter L. Bergen, *The Osama bin Laden I Know: An Oral History of Al-Qaeda's Leader* (New York: Free Press, 2006), 321–22; Bruce Lawrence, ed., *Messages to the World: The Statements of Osama bin Laden,* trans. James Howarth (London: Verso, 2005), 140–41.

13. Michael Walzer, *Just and Unjust Wars: A Moral Argument with Historical Illustrations,* 3rd ed. (New York: Basic Books, 2000), 19.

Chapter 8

1. For a good discussion of the costs of lying for a society, see Evelin Sullivan, *The Concise Book of Lying* (New York: Farrar, Straus and Giroux, 2001), 55–147.

2. Francis Fukuyama, *Trust: The Social Virtues and The Creation of Prosperity* (New York: Free Press, 1995); Luigi Guiso, Paola Sapienza, Luigi Zingales, "The Role of Social Capital in Financial Development" (working paper 7563, National Bureau of Economic Research, February 2000); Marc J. Hetherington, *Why Trust Matters: Declining Political Trust and the Demise of American Liberalism*

(Princeton, NJ: Princeton University Press, 2005); Stephen Knack and Philip Keefer, "Does Social Capital Have an Economic Payoff? A Cross-Country Investigation," *Quarterly Journal of Economics* 112, no. 4 (November 1997): 1251–88; Rafael La Porta et al., "Trust in Large Organizations," *American Economic Review* 87, no. 2 (May 1997): 333–38; Robert D. Putnam, *Making Democracy Work: Civic Traditions in Modern Italy* (Princeton, NJ: Princeton University Press, 1993); Charles Tilly, *Trust and Rule* (New York: Cambridge University Press, 2005).

3. "Transcript of Special Counsel Fitzgerald's Press Conference," *Washington Post,* October 28, 2005. The best book about the Libby case is Michael Isikoff and David Corn, *Hubris: The Inside Story of Spin, Scandal, and the Selling of the Iraq War* (New York: Crown, 2006).

4. Ken Armstrong and Steve Mills, "Death Row Justice Derailed," *Chicago Tribune,* November 14, 1999; Ken Armstrong and Steve Mills, "Inept Defenses Cloud Verdict," *Chicago Tribune,* November 15, 1999; Ken Armstrong and Steve Mills, "The Jailhouse Informant," *Chicago Tribune,* November 16, 1999; Ken Armstrong and Steve Mills, "A Tortured Path to Death Row," *Chicago Tribune,* November 17, 1999; Ken Armstrong and Steve Mills, "Convicted by a Hair," *Chicago Tribune,* November 18, 1999; Martha Irvine, "Illinois Governor Orders Death Penalty Moratorium," Associated Press, January 31, 2000; Barry James, "Clearing of Illinois Death Row Is Greeted with Global Cheers," *New York Times,* January 14, 2003; Paul M. Krawzak, "Ryan Explains Moratorium Call," Copley News Service, January 31, 2000; Robert E. Pierre and Kari Lydersen, "Illinois Death Row Emptied," *Washington Post,* January 12, 2003.

5. Dwight D. Eisenhower, *Waging Peace, 1956–1961: The White House Years* (Garden City, NY: Doubleday, 1965), chap. 23; Peter Lyon, *Eisenhower: Portrait of the Hero* (Boston: Little, Brown, 1974), 859–66.

6. See Andrew T. Guzmán, *How International Law Works: A Rational Choice Theory* (New York: Oxford University Press, 2008), especially chap. 3.

7. Ann E. Sartori argues that "states often are tempted to bluff, or dissemble, but a state that is caught bluffing acquires a reputation for doing so, and opponents are less likely to believe its future communications." Thus, states usually do not bluff or lie, because of the damage it might do to their reputation, and thus their prospects

for future cooperation. "The prospect of acquiring a reputation for lying—and lessening the credibility of the state's future diplomacy—keeps statesmen and diplomats honest except when fibs are the most tempting." *Deterrence by Diplomacy* (Princeton, NJ: Princeton University Press, 2005), 5. I agree that reputation matters a lot to states in the realm of low politics and that this discourages lying, but, contrary to Sartori, I do not think reputation is important when dealing with matters relating to high politics. See Daryl G. Press, *Calculating Credibility: How Leaders Assess Military Threats* (Ithaca, NY: Cornell University Press, 2005).

8. As John M. Schuessler makes clear, however, Roosevelt's deceptions in the run-up to the war with Japan did impede his conduct of the war in a variety of ways. "The Deception Dividend," *International Security* 34, no. 4 (Spring 2010): 162–63. See also Thomas J. Christensen, *Useful Adversaries: Grand Strategy, Domestic Mobilization, and Sino-American Conflict, 1947–1958* (Princeton, N.J.: Princeton University Press, 1996).

9. George Orwell, *Orwell and Politics: Animal Farm in the Context of Essays, Reviews and Letters Selected from the Complete Works of George Orwell,* ed. Peter Davison (London: Penguin, 2001), 357. Orwell also wrote, "The nationalist not only does not disapprove of atrocities committed by his own side, but has a remarkable capacity for not even hearing about them" (ibid., 363).

10. Richard E. Neustadt, *Presidential Power: The Politics of Leadership* (New York: New American Library, 1964), 134.

11. P. M. Kennedy, "The Decline of Nationalistic History in the West, 1900–1970," *Journal of Contemporary History* 8, no. 1 (January 1973): 77–100; Stephen Van Evera, "Primed for Peace: Europe After the Cold War," *International Security* 15, no. 3 (Winter 1990/1991): 23–25; Stephen Van Evera, "Hypotheses on Nationalism and War," *International Security* 18, no. 4 (Spring 1994). See also Holger H. Herwig, "Clio Deceived: Patriotic Self-Censorship in Germany after the Great War," *International Security* 12, no. 2 (Fall 1987): 5–44.

12. Dale C. Copeland, *The Origins of Major War* (Ithaca, NY: Cornell University Press, 2000), chaps. 3–4; John J. Mearsheimer, *The Tragedy of Great Power Politics* (New York: Norton, 2001), 181–90.

13. John J. Mearsheimer and Stephen M. Walt, *The Israel Lobby and U.S. Foreign Policy* (New York: Farrar, Straus and Giroux, 2007), 92–97.

14. Works that emphasize both the nationalist and realist sides of Bismarck's foreign policy between 1862 and 1870 are: Lothar Gall, *Bismarck: The White Revolutionary,* trans. J. A. Underwood (Boston: Allen & Unwin, 1986); Bruce Waller, *Bismarck,* 2nd ed. (Oxford: Blackwell, 1997), chaps. 2–4; Otto Pflanze, *Bismarck and the Development of Germany: The Period of Unification, 1815–1871* (Princeton, NJ: Princeton University Press, 1973).

Chapter 9

1. Minxin Pei, *China's Trapped Transition: The Limits of Developmental Autocracy* (Cambridge, MA: Harvard University Press, 2006).

Index